ALASTAIR BURNET · WILLIE LANDELS

THE TIME OF OUR LIVES

A pictorial history of Britain since 1945

Elm Tree Books
London

First published in Great Britain 1981
by Elm Tree Books/Hamish Hamilton Ltd
Garden House 57–59 Long Acre London WC2E 9JZ

British Library Cataloguing in Publication Data

Burnet, Alastair
    The time of our lives.
    1. Great Britain – History – George VI, 1936–52 – Pictorial works
    2. Great Britain – History – Elizabeth II, 1952–   – Pictorial works
    I. Title   II. Landels, Willie
    941.085   DA588

ISBN 0-241-10666-4

Typeset by CCC, printed and bound in Great Britain by
William Clowes (Beccles) Limited, Beccles and London

This book was designed and produced by
John Calmann and Cooper Ltd, London

Acknowledgements

The author and John Calmann and Cooper Ltd would like to thank the following agencies and photographers who supplied the illustrations for this book.

Allsport Photographic: 70 (bottom left). **British Rail:** 51. **Camera Press Ltd:** 22 (Oliver Waterlow), 36 (top right), 38 (bottom), 99 (Lewis Morley; bottom), 108 (top right), 117 (top), 126, 127 (centre), 128–129, 140, 145 (T. Spencer; bottom), 150 (bottom), 151 (top), 153 (top), 155 (right), 160 (bottom), 162 (centre left), 164, 166, 168–169, 171, 174 (top), 178 (bottom left), 180 (bottom right), 184, 191 (Lionel Cherruault; top), 199 (Lionel Cherruault), 203 (Mike Wells; top), 206 (Ian Swift). **Central Press Ltd:** 8, 13, 15, 19, 27, 28, 37 (bottom), 38 (top), 44, 57 (right), 58 (bottom), 63 (centre), 80, 81, 88 (bottom), 119 (top), 120 (top), 137 (top right, bottom), 155 (bottom), 157, 186 (right), 191 (bottom left), 193 (bottom), 195 (right), 202 (top), 203 (bottom), 204 (bottom). **Colorific:** 6. **Crown Copyright:** 132 (top left). **EMI Films Ltd:** 16 (top). **Elisabeth:** 16 (bottom), 135 (right). **Fox Photos Ltd:** 4, 9 (bottom), 10 (top), 11, 34 (top), 37 (top right), 41 (bottom), 46 (top), 51 (top), 54, 55 (bottom), 58 (top right), 61 (bottom), 63, 64 (top), 65, 67 (top right, bottom left), 68, 69 (top), 72 (bottom), 75 (bottom), 78 (top), 83 (top), 86 (bottom centre), 87, 90 (bottom right), 91 (bottom left), 93 (top), 105 (bottom), 120 (bottom), 139 (bottom right), 143 (top right). **Fay Godwin:** 136. **Harpers & Queen:** 13. **Keystone Press Agency Ltd:** 25, 36 (top left, bottom left, bottom centre), 37 (top left), 42 (top), 45 (bottom), 47 (top left), 50, 59 (top), 61 (top), 64 (bottom), 66 (top right, bottom), 67 (top left, bottom right), 69 (bottom), 71, 76 (bottom), 78 (bottom), 82 (top), 86 (top), 91 (top), 98, 101 (top), 103 (bottom right), 111, 115 (bottom), 117 (top), 121 (top), 123, 125 (top), 132 (right), 135 (top left), 142, 143 (top left), 145 (top, top right), 150 (top), 152 (bottom), 156, 160 (top), 161 (top), 162 (bottom left), 165, 172 (top), 173, 175 (bottom), 176 (bottom), 178 (top, bottom right), 179 (top), 181, 183 (top), 186 (left), 186–187, 187, 189, 191 (bottom right), 196, 197 (bottom), 202 (bottom), 205. **Michel Molinare:** 43 (bottom). **Popperfoto:** 30–31, 32–33, 35 (top), 40, 51 (bottom), 52 (right), 60, 66 (left), 70 (bottom centre), 76 (bottom), 79 (top), 84 (top right), 88 (top), 89 (bottom), 90 (top), 92 (top), 100 (bottom), 103 (top left), 104 (bottom left), 108 (bottom right), 112, 116 (top), 119 (centre), 122 (top), 137 (top left), 138 (top), 143 (bottom left), 146, 148 (bottom), 151 (bottom), 153 (bottom), 163 (top), 167, 175 (top), 188 (right). **Press Association:** 62 (bottom right), 79 (bottom), 86 (centre), 104 (top, bottom right), 110 (top), 113, 114, 121 (botto,n), 131 (left), 147 (top), 149 (top), 152 (bottom), 161 (bottom), 172 (bottom), 174 (bottom), 176 (centre), 192, 200 (bottom), 201. **Rex Features Ltd:** 91 (bottom right), 92 (bottom right), 93 (bottom left), 125 (bottom), 134 (left, bottom right), 158–159, 162 (top left and right), 170, 180 (left), 183 (bottom). **S & G Press Agency Ltd:** 9 (top), 47 (bottom), 77 (top centre), 188 (left). **Frank Spooner Pictures:** 14, 182, 190 (top), 197 (top), 204 (top), 207 (top). **Syndication International:** 5, 10 (bottom), 24, 29, 35 (bottom), 36 (bottom right), 43 (top), 46 (bottom), 47 (top right), 53 (top), 59 (bottom), 62 (bottom left), 72 (top), 73, 74 (top), 75 (top), 77 (top left), 82 (bottom), 84 (left, bottom right), 85, 86 (bottom left), 92 (bottom left), 93 (bottom right), 94, 95, 96, 97, 99 (top), 100 (top), 101 (bottom), 103 (top right), 105 (top), 106–107, 108 (left), 109, 110 (bottom), 119 (bottom), 124, 127 (top, bottom), 131 (top, bottom), 134 (top right), 138 (bottom), 139 (bottom left), 141, 147 (bottom), 148 (top), 149 (bottom, centre), 154, 168, 169, 177 (left), 185, 190 (bottom), 193 (top), 194, 195 (left), 198, 200 (top), 204 (centre), 207 (bottom). **The Tate Gallery, London:** 7, 179 (bottom). **The Times:** 57 (left), 70 (bottom right), 74 (top), 132 (bottom left), 133. **John Topham Picture Library:** 34 (bottom), 39, 41 (top), 42 (bottom), 45 (top), 47 (centre), 48–49, 52 (left), 53 (bottom), 55, 58 (top left), 62 (bottom), 77 (top, bottom), 83 (bottom right), 86 (bottom right), 89 (top), 90 (bottom left), 102, 110 (right), 115 (top), 116 (bottom), 118, 122 (bottom), 126, 130, 139 (top), 143 (bottom right). **United Artists Corporation Ltd:** 163 (bottom). **Yorkshire Post:** 176 (top), 177 (right).
Cover: Central Press Ltd (1970 Derby, Concorde, Virginia Wade, Margaret Thatcher); EMI Records Ltd (The Beatles); Fox Photos Ltd (Princess Anne's wedding); Keystone Press Agency Ltd (HM The Queen, 1966 World Cup, Winston Churchill, demonstration, Union Jack); Time-Life (mini-skirt).

Contents

THEY HAVE NOT been the best of times for us; nor quite the worst. In just 35 years, half a man's lifetime, we have seen our horizons shrink at a speed that would have astounded our fathers. We knew, in the rejoicing and the relief of VE day in 1945, that Britain was no longer, as it had been on Armistice day 1918, the strongest and the wealthiest nation on earth.

But Britain still thought of itself as one of the war's three victorious powers with its armies and fleets astride three continents. In the new peace it expected its influence, as Winston Churchill conceived it, to be as strong as ever and exerted in three decisive relationships: with the United States and the English-speaking world, with the developing Commonwealth, and with an appreciative and united Europe. That independent role was as much in the mind of Labour's foreign secretary, Ernest Bevin, as it was in Churchill's.

Today, 56 million of us find ourselves a middling sort of power on a middling-sized island, enjoying an economic prosperity something like that available in East Germany and Czechoslovakia.

Outwardly, this does not worry us very much. Our politicians find us hard to arouse; and we have been deserting the political parties in droves. We are suspicious of dogma; we are used to muddling through. Many of us are placidly unaware of, or flatly do not believe, the statistics of our decline.

From the Americans we expect to get courtesy, occasional help and, every ten years or so, a sophisticated and expensive nuclear weapons system. The Commonwealth is a place from which black immigrants come, or used to come. We know we are in Europe; we also know we are still not of it.

We like to grumble, but most of us are now pretty comfortable. We may be among the worst-paid people in western Europe, but we are also high among the best-housed. Too little has been invested in too much of British industry, but there is oil in the North Sea. We make it seem that we lost the empire, as it was won, in a fit of absentmindedness. But even when it was not a deliberate policy, the dismantling was unrivalled in efficiency and bloodlessness. In August 1947 Rajendra Prasad, president of the assembly in newly-independent India, called it 'the consummation of the democratic ideals of the British race'. And India, at least, is still a democracy.

Parliament in question.
The Commons are summoned by Black Rod
to hear the Queen's Speech
after Labour's electoral sweep in 1966. Wilson's
front bench (left of the table) still has
the former transport union leader,
Frank Cousins, on it.
Cousins's resignation, against
the austerity measures of that July,
exemplified even Labour politicians'
inability to satisfy the unions.

The last of Churchill.
Guarded by senior officers
of the services in turn
(right, the navy),
the body of Sir Winston Churchill
lay in state at Westminister Hall
after his death on 24 January 1965.
Queues miles long stretched
along the Embankment through the night
to file past in farewell.

To anyone who still listens, we complain that we are now too comfortable, too imperturbable, too stable, too lazy. And that is, indeed, widely believed around the world, especially among ambassadors.

The truth is different. We are, as we have always been, a cussed and contrary people, but quite cleverly so. We have preserved (and are secretly proud that we have) a comforting political stability. We are as unlikely to give it up as we are to give up the monarchy. This does not remove the politics of envy or the residuums of the class war, but it helps contain them. Of course, it angers those who still seek to impose irreversible changes of their own on society.

We have kept, too, a broadly liberal and voluntary outlook on our affairs. Again it makes us, fortunately, difficult to govern. It means the police have a harder time getting convictions than they would like; but it has made them better policemen than in any other country. Most of them are still unarmed. It means it is increasingly hard to dump nuclear waste in the hills, pollute rivers, drown valleys, or pour concrete for unnecessary motorways. This irritates authority because it is against progress, but the British have always suspected there are sorts of progress that it is wise to be against. We like having things both ways. It means the welfare state itself, now something of an invalid, is helped and made more human by countless charities.

Britain still has an enviable stock of education and of educational apparatus and skills. It may still be unrivalled in scientific and inventive ability. The Nobel prize lists suggest this is so. Indeed, it has been our very liveliness that regularly surprises our friends, and sometimes ourselves.

The post-war British have sailed single-handed round the world. We organized the first expedition to reach the top of Everest. We won, or at least the English won, soccer's World Cup. We produced the first man to run a mile in under four minutes, and world champions in most things from Formula 1 motor racing to flyweight boxing. The Beatles were ours. So was swinging London. So is the glory of the London stage and of London's music.

If we were just too comfortable or too lazy we would not be beyond redemption. But we have made things harder for ourselves than that. We do not admit it, but it is precisely because we are still an ingenious and capable people that we have actually tried just about everything to better ourselves in the past 35 years; but we have never given anything time to work properly. We have taken up each nostrum and dropped it by turns. Eighteen months is about all that public opinion and governments have allowed any policy before announcing, often petulantly, that it does not work miracles.

The British economy has been given go-stop-go-stop orders by successive chancellors of the two big parties. Since the war 15 chancellors (average time in office, two years four months), their faces wrenched into smiles, have appeared on the steps of No. 11 Downing Street and held up the battered red budget box for all the world to see as if it contained coherent, consistent policies. Too often they have known that their forecasts might already be out of date, and that the measures most concerning them are no more inspiring than tuppence on a pint of beer. The ambitious chancellors go for growth. The frightened ones say stop. Often enough it has been the same

Pop goes painting.
Something had to give in British painting
and, appropriately in 1961, give it did.
The Young Contemporaries exhibition knocked the critics over
and gave lift-off to the dizzy career and works of David Hockney
(above: *Man Taking a Shower in Beverly Hills*, 1964).

All you need is Beatles. The famous four
(ascending, left: Ringo, Paul, George and John) emerged from the Cavern Club
in Liverpool, helped by their percipient manager, Brian Epstein,
to project the country into the singing 'sixties
and make themselves millionaires.
By the 1970s they were acrimoniously apart.
In December 1980, John Lennon was shot dead in New York.

man. As the economy, unsurprisingly, has slid into stagflation, the goes have become increasingly rash and the stops increasingly harsh.

There is potential for a lot of ruin in a country, but too many British chancellors have come close to finding out just how much. All were men of ability. Three of them (Gaitskell, Macmillan, Callaghan) eventually led their parties; almost all the others aspired to. Only one, Roy Jenkins, left with his reputation higher than when he began. Perhaps most of them, and their advisers at the Treasury and the Bank of England, were just too clever by half.

For lengthy periods, especially 1945–49 and 1964–67, the value of the pound sterling was desperately defended against speculation—at great cost to plain people in terms of unemployment and lost output—when it was plainly too high against other currencies, especially the dollar, deutschemark and yen. Prime ministers and the Bank of England discouraged any talk of devaluation. Wilson even burned the advice he got. Chancellors denied it would happen until after the last moment. But the £1 came down, just the same, all the way from $4.03 to $2.40.

The Conservatives then pushed the rate up again to $2.48 at the Smithsonian agreement in 1971, but within a year decided a floating pound was better. Then Labour, in 1974–76, tried a totally different tack. Going on another theory, the £1 was encouraged to collapse, to help exports. It obediently fell all the way to $1.56½ on 27 October 1976. The result was panic and the biggest-ever drawing on the International Monetary Fund: $3,900 million, in January

Growing up. The royal family gathered at Balmoral, as usual, in the summer of 1972
(not in the picture: Princess Anne), the year of the silver wedding celebrations.
The boys were plainly shooting up fast,
though Prince Charles was not yet actively contemplating matrimony.

1977. The Conservatives, on their return in 1979, promptly drove the pound up again, this time to cut the cost of imports.

Taxation, too, has been bewilderingly chopped and changed. The highest income taxes in the developed world have been slapped on the wealthy (in 1951, 19s 6d in the £1 on income above £20,000), and then taken off. Company taxes have been stiff when governments have wanted to woo the trade unions; then, when the same governments have got into a mess over investment, company taxes have become almost non-existent.

All that has been consistent, under Labour more than Conservative chancellors, has been the spread of income tax to millions of families that never paid it before.

The rise of inflation has been consistent,

Cricket's rebellion.
Unhappy over pay, England's captain,
Tony Greig (above, against
the Australians at Trent Bridge, 1977),
and several of his better professionals
signed to play for the Kerry Packer
world cricket series. Greig did well
for himself, some of the others not so well.
Cricket was never quite the same again.

England, their England. To the delight and relief of Wembley,
England (Hurst 3, Peters) beat West Germany 4–2 in the World Cup final in 1966.
But the Germans (below, scoring despite the endeavours of Charlton J., Stiles and Banks) took them to the
inconvenience of extra time.

The mini generation.
It began in Mary Quant's Bazaar,
in the King's Road, Chelsea,
and, once seen, was never forgotten.
Within months the mini skirt had captured
a generation around the world and started
a multi-million-pound business.
Later from Quant:
hipster pants and skinny-rib sweaters,
both good tries.

Loyal to the royals.
They put up the flags and brought out
the tables in the mean streets
to celebrate the Queen's
silver jubilee in 1977.
That was after they had seen the
televised service at St Paul's first.
Street parties celebrate royal occasions
and other important things
like the end of wars;
they are not thrown for politicians.

too. Inflation was rising by over 20 per cent in 1975 and 1980, on both occasions after new governments had been elected promising not to control wages. But all governments have come to wage controls one way or another.

There have been statutory incomes policies, voluntary incomes policies (and the same for prices), freezes, pauses, plateaus, social contracts, guiding lights, three wise men, stage ones, stage twos, thresholds, each and every device and palliative that bright civil servants have been able to think up. Then, for only brief moments, there has been nothing at all.

Over the years it has meant that governments, usually for the best of motives, have fought the unions in every known way to hold down wages, and have then let wages rip. The incomes-policy men say their efforts have helped to avoid the worst. The monetarists say it has all been irrelevant; they have the only cure. That cure is now being put to the test.

Governments have tried to reform industrial relations and union practices; then they put the unions above the law, then tried to pull them down again. It has invariably ended with the governments coming spectacular croppers. In 1969 Wilson and his employment secretary, Barbara Castle, were forced to retreat over *In Place of Strife* with its proposals for a 28-day conciliation period and for secret ballots before certain strikes. The unions, much of the Labour party and, in the cabinet, James Callaghan, saw to that.

The Heath government's industrial relations act was duly defied by the dockers. It took the Court of Appeal and, later, a person called the Official Solicitor, not so much to save union officials and men from prison, as to save the government's face. After 1974 the Labour government gave the unions mostly what they asked for, only to find the strikers and flying pickets in the

Prince of Wales.
The Queen presented her eldest son
to the people of Wales on 1 July 1969,
a damp day which had started
with the odd extremist bomb. But despite,
or because of, the nationalists' disfavour,
most of Wales seemed to enjoy it.

Queen

FIVE SHILLINGS

ENGLAND IS...

CHRISTMAS ISSUE

Style, actually.
The Christmas issue of *Queen* in 1967
told the English (and some Scots and Welsh too, no doubt)
just what they had to be proud of. It had to be some time ago:
the price, five shillings (25p), was in the old money
before decimalization and inflation really caught on.

The iron lady. Margaret Thatcher was elected Britain's
first woman prime minister on 3–4 May 1979, and so sweeping was her victory
that the computers got it right from the start.
She promptly gave the electors the medicine she thought good for them.

winter of discontent, 1978–79, the prime instigators of its downfall.

And governments have changed their attitudes to unemployment. Throughout the 1950s the Conservatives kept unemployment down, artificially, because they had been blamed for the unemployment of the 1930s and had paid the price electorally. Indeed, for 20 years up to 1966, unemployment was below 2.5 per cent.

In the late 1960s and the 1970s Labour let unemployment rise, chiefly because it was frightened of the International Monetary Fund, to which Labour chancellors were regularly in debt. Even so, as late as the summer of 1979 unemployment in Britain was only just above five per cent. Under Margaret Thatcher's monetarism it then doubled.

Unemployment reacted to world booms and recessions, and its impact on families was alleviated by social security. The 1930s were still far away. Yet once again it seemed that Britain had contrived to end up with the worst of arrangements.

The highly successful effort to keep unemployment down in the 1950s, even below normal turnover in the labour market, left the economy in south-east England and the Midlands badly strained (it was called 'over-heated') whenever political convenience or Keynesian theory called for a little stimulus.

By contrast, the soaring figures of 1979–81 began to encourage disillusionment and demos (especially by young blacks) when-

ever monetarist theory dictated that the chancellor must keep the screws on. The work force that had had it too easy for too long, as the employers said, now found their employers complaining that good firms were going to the wall and would not recover again. The signals were all confusing to plain people; they were, of course, the ones who got hurt, especially in northern England, Scotland and Wales which had never known 'over-heating' at all.

Consistency in politicians is not necessarily a virtue; nor inconsistency a vice. But British politicians have blandly claimed consistency throughout, while behaving quite otherwise. No doubt they hoped for too much, especially after the war, and promised too much, especially before elections; naturally we, their electorates, would never be fobbed off with modest promises. So things went wrong.

The National Health Service, our brave post-war present to ourselves, was going to cost no more in 1965 than it did in 1945 according to Lord Beveridge's original estimate. Then, quite quickly, it was costing a whole lot more. Teeth and spectacles were going to be free; then they weren't. This put a particular strain on Labour. Wilson followed Bevan out of the Labour cabinet in 1951 because Gaitskell's budget began charges for prescriptions and false teeth. The Wilson government, after devaluation in 1967, put up charges for prescriptions, teeth and spectacles, and went even further. It ended free milk in secondary schools and postponed raising the school-leaving age from 15 to 16.

For years, the whole welfare state, after receiving a declining proportion of the country's wealth, has been going visibly broke. Social security payments began to cost more than defence, which some people liked and some did not like; but as payment for both rose inexorably, and working-class taxes too, it was the cost and the bureaucracy of the social services that got most of the stick. There was a state pension fund, then another, then another, then yet another.

Secondary education, under the 1944 Act, began by being selective; this was thought to be a great step forward. Then, as

Belfast burns. Troops went in to keep rioting Catholics and Protestants apart
in Northern Ireland in August 1969.
The authorities said they would restore law and order and
'will be withdrawn as soon as this is accomplished'.
They are still there.

the middle class rebelled against the 11-plus exam, it started to be locally, and experimentally, non-selective. By the late 1960s, on social as much as on educational grounds, it was turning compulsorily comprehensive. This was stopped in 1970, restarted in 1974, and stopped again in 1979. No wonder there was a boom in independent schools.

Unlimited numbers of black immigrants from the Commonwealth were officially accepted, even welcomed, into the British economy and community until 1962. Then the Conservatives put on limited controls, which Labour opposed. Then the Kenya Asians moved in, and the Labour government stopped them in 1968. Then the

Uganda Asians were expelled by Idi Amin, and the Conservative government took them in. Then almost all black immigration was stopped. Then the Labour party conference began voting to repeal all the Immigration Acts—except the original Conservative one.

Britain's foreign policy began by having nothing whatsoever to do with the European Common Market. Britain was then twice rejected and humiliated when the Conservatives tried to join in 1962 and Labour in 1967. We got in at last in 1972 with unreal hopes and promises. After only minor changes, we voted two-to-one in the referendum of 1975 to stay in. By 1980 there were moves in the Labour party to take us

Embassy siege. The Iranian embassy in London,
seized with 22 hostages by gunmen in May 1980, was stormed by the SAS.
All the hostages were rescued (above, a BBC man who was held leaves the hard way)
and all but one of the gunmen were shot.
It was seen live on television, the best viewing of the year.

out again, without a referendum.

British defence policy has oscillated sharply and expensively between preparing for a big European war and dealing with counter-insurgency in Northern Ireland; between east of Suez and west of Suez; between going back into Suez itself and getting out of almost all overseas bases; between a conscript and a professional army; between priority for an independent nuclear deterrent and priority for conventional warfare.

Most of these shifts in policy, or at least in what official policy was supposed to be, made little sense to people who did not follow the political game at all closely. To

the politicians behind them they were, of course, the triumphs and failures of their careers.

Most politicians of any ability seemed to believe that their real opponents were not sitting directly opposite them in the House of Commons but were dispersed around Whitehall and in the big government departments farther afield. It was the power of the civil service (over whose recruitment, appointment and inner processes the politicians had little or no control) which appeared to give a continuity, or at least a recognizable drift, to certain national policies.

The Treasury was known to be against devaluations and for incomes policies. The

Foreign Office was known to be for joining the Common Market and staying in it; and the Ministry of Agriculture for staying out. Each ministry has had its predilections and its clientele. Labour politicians, Tony Benn and Crossman especially, have felt their civil servants were keeping things from them, and plotting to nullify their policy changes.

These complaints may be exaggerated. Even so, the authority and unaccountability of the civil service have contrived to bring some apparent order and shape into the conduct of affairs that would otherwise have been even more at the mercy of sharply differing political programmes. Naturally enough, that outward sense of order has often come about by the bureaucracy changing little and doing little, except, of course, inflating its own size and remuneration.

The ballet boom.
The Royal Ballet's international success
helped to persuade the taxpayers that
they liked paying for it after all.
Some of it was very British.
The *Tales of Beatrix Potter* had
Michael Coleman dancing as Jeremy Fisher,
and it was shown on the telly too.

It's our oil. The discovery of oil under the North Sea
and its increasing arrival on shore in the later 1970s
gave the economy a breather. Balance of payments worries receded.
But it also meant a high pound,
with problems for manufacturing exporters.
Still, if it was so bad having it, what would happen when it ran out?

Some of these confusions, contradictions and failures happened through muddle-headedness, some of them through just playing politics. There was opportunism and there was cynicism. There was bad luck, too. But the intellectual effort and financial investment put into each new policy were substantial.

Through most of the years we have spent more of our wealth on defence than any of our European allies. We spent as high a proportion on research and development as almost any other country in the world. We doubled the money we spent on health and doubled the number of doctors and nurses. We nearly trebled our universities. We spent more on education than on anything else, and although we did not catch up with other industrialized countries, we tried. In the 1950s one child in ten stayed on at school to the age of 17 or 18. In the 1970s one in four did.

So why the sense of failure? Did we really try too hard?

Through all the years when the politicians were demanding that everything be tried once, twice or thrice to put the country's affairs to rights, we have been encouraged to see Britain, however weakened by disappointment, as still an influential country in the world.

If Britain were to be shifted from its present allies, or neutralized, or even to renounce nuclear weapons, it would be seen to be a stunning blow to the western alliance and the entire balance of power.

If Britain were to change the nature of its society and economy into something closer to the life of the socialist countries in eastern Europe, it would be seen as a momentous signal for democracies everywhere.

If Britain were even to give up the last of its influence, its credit, its appeal in the corners of the world where it was once dominant, it would be said that a vital element on the world's agenda, and in those countries' own expectations, had been lost.

Or so we often think. There must be something that matters left for us to do.

We were never as insulted by de Gaulle over Europe or by Nasser over Suez or by Mossadeq over Iranian oil as we were by Dean Acheson saying at West Point in December 1962, 'Great Britain has lost an empire and has not yet found a role'. A friend should have known that we are never at any loss for a role.

What countries think of themselves should always be taken seriously. Even if it is illusion, or partly illusion, it is likely to motivate their actions and their aspirations. It is this sense of our own importance that has seemed to add an extra weight to our burdens, to the hastiness with which policies have been changed or dropped, and to the intensity with which political rivalry has been fought out.

Labour's election victory in July 1945 was a sweeping one. It had a majority of 146 over all other parties in the Commons, bigger than anyone was to get again. Labour talked in those heady days as if it were a revolution: the first socialist government to come to real power in Britain. The young Hartley Shawcross, newly-elected, declared, 'We are the masters ... for a very long time to come'. Churchill himself, in his first election broadcast, had used apocalyptic words, 'Socialism is inseparably interwoven with totalitarianism ... they would have to fall back on some form of Gestapo'.

There was never, of course, a less revolutionary socialist than the prime minister, Attlee—unless it were the dominant members of his cabinet: Bevin, Dalton and Morrison. There was, indeed, a wartime coalition programme to bring in a welfare state, based on Beveridge's report. The Tories accepted, almost without demur, the nationalization of the coal mines and railways, though the future of steel, partly because it was not brought forward until near the end of the government's term, was found to be highly ideological. In other lands at other times it might all have passed off with a minimum of friction.

But those were exciting times. The USSR's motives were distrusted. Churchill, at Fulton, Missouri, saw 'an iron curtain descend across Europe'. In 1948 there was a communist coup in Czechoslovakia. Britain, France and the Benelux countries signed the Brussels treaty, the first military pact against communism. The Soviets blockaded West Berlin, and the Americans and British organized an air-lift to keep it alive. Britain seemed again to be at the centre of what might shortly be the third world war.

As Labour failed to get exports and investment moving as quickly as the trade gap demanded, as the American loan ran out alarmingly, as even bread and potatoes were restricted (as they had not been in the war), there was a new edge to the political debate on where socialism would lead the country.

It was so important a debate that it divided Labour and led directly to its exclusion from office for 13 years. The Attlee leadership welcomed (indeed, had prompted) Marshall aid from America and the Nato alliance. It decided to make the British atom bomb, sent a force to help the United Nations in Korea when the north invaded the south in 1950, and adopted a rearmament programme costing £4,700 million—which was the breaking point for Nye Bevan and the left because it was at the expense of the welfare state. It was a split kept open by the prolonged argument over West German rearmament. Into it were drawn all the animosities and divisions of left and right, not least of them the rivalry between Bevan and Gaitskell. It was nearly fatal to the party.

The years of Conservative rule after 1951 brought together the Labour right under Gaitskell and the Tory left under Butler in an unspoken understanding about the Keynesian priorities of economic policy. This was called Butskellism, and the sense of continuity it engendered coincided with the economy's best post-war performance in investment and growth. But it angered the Labour left still more, and the Tory right, too; and it was vulnerable, not just to the vicissitudes of world trade, but to the demands of Britain's international role. That nearly proved fatal, too, and not just to the Conservatives.

Eden ordered the British intervention at Suez in 1956 without the Americans, believing that the Middle East was still a British sphere of influence, that Nasser was a threat to British interests comparable to Mussolini in the 1930s, and that Britain and France had the power to impose their will.

This divided the country politically, although he probably had the majority behind him, but what stopped the intervention in its tracks before the canal could be taken was not political but economic: a run on sterling that could not be withstood. Eden, warned by his chancellor, Macmillan, promptly halted the operation. A small war had bankrupted the country overnight. The lesson was not lost on Macmillan, particularly. The retreat from empire was speeded up. The old role was simply too expensive.

Macmillan now embarked on a rapid, and broadly successful, withdrawal from Africa. His words to the South African parliament in February 1960, 'the wind of change is blowing through this continent', set the pace for decolonization. But his colonial secretary, Iain Macleod, took the brunt of the imperialist wing's disgruntlement. He was, said Salisbury, 'too clever by half' and the right dug in to keep Rhodesia white.

Even so, Macmillan was readily persuaded that international diplomacy was still the real job of a British prime minister. Despite his stunning election victory in 1959 (a majority of 100), he paid little enough attention to the economy or the unions until it was nearly too late. His mind was on summitry, on the alliance, on the nuclear test ban treaty that was signed in 1963. It pleased him to reassert (and it pleased President Kennedy to let him) Britain's place at the top table and to renew the special relationship between Washington and London for another decade. It might have been wiser if his special relationship had been with de Gaulle.

Macmillan's brief successor, Douglas-Home, was not the man to discourage ideas of Britain's continuing importance. Foreign policy was the job he knew best. Indeed, he had two modest successes east of Suez to suggest that Britain did still matter there: the rescue of the new East African governments from insurrection, and the start of British support for Malaysia against Indonesia.

Nor was Wilson, once he had arrived at No. 10, the man to withdraw from anything or anywhere if he could help it. He enjoyed diplomacy and repeatedly tried to mediate in the Vietnam war. He spent much time on

Rhodesia after UDI in 1965. He kept the nuclear deterrent. He spoke of Britain's frontier being along the Himalayas. At the least this was massively distracting; at worst it made withdrawal from east of Suez, and especially from the Gulf, damagingly ill-judged in its timing and hurried in its execution. But when it happened Britain could not afford to do anything else.

The search for a role, one fitting for a once-great power, now narrowed down to Europe. There was an economic argument for going into the Common Market, but it was by no means a clear-cut one to those who understood how debilitated the British economy was becoming; anyway it was thought that so momentous a decision needed to be dignified above bargaining over groceries.

So it was put about that Britain would lead Europe, that it would be in the technological forefront in Europe, and that this new Europe would become the equal of the super-powers in population, wealth, power and influence. Against this Gaitskell, the most thoughtful of all the Common Market's opponents, spoke of 'the end of a thousand years of history', and Enoch Powell has tried to regenerate a distinctive English patriotism.

The result has been unhappy. France would not risk British leadership in Europe, which de Gaulle knew would be American, until after Britain was palpably too anaemic to assert any such thing. Heath, after more than a decade of trying to get in, paid too high a financial price to open the door in 1972; the efforts of Callaghan and, rather more successfully, Thatcher to renegotiate entry have increased distrust and division.

The Europe of the nine has been slow to develop politically, and even slower to correct weaknesses such as the common agricultural policy, so that much of Britain has become disillusioned and ready to talk about withdrawal. Our policy and hopes have fallen, once again, between illusion and reality.

There are many explanations, many excuses. Those dedicated to the class conflict put that in the forefront; they say nothing about, for example, the technical success of

The indestructible.
At least the sculptor Henry Moore was honoured in his own country.
His work, monumental and immediately recognizable, became essential to every pretentious new building in London, which occasionally worried so modest a man, but he was out with his umbrella to supervise the 1978 exhibition in Kensington Gardens on his 80th birthday.

British farming which now claims virtually the highest investment and productivity in the world. Those who blame the monopoly bargaining power of trade unions are silent about the quality of life that the existence of a national health service guarantees. Those most enthusiastic about a post-industrial society do not travel often to Clydeside or Merseyside.

The safest conclusion is that much of our experience since the war is not peculiar to us; it is happening now in most advanced industrial societies. What has mattered is that it has happened in Britain first.

Britain has been first in the growth of the public sector in industry. When and where this has been at the expense of the private sector and has reduced profitability because of high taxes, Britain has been first in failing to invest in new industry in the private sector. So over two million jobs have been taken out of manufacturing in 15 years.

Britain has often been first in raising wages, both in employees' pay packets and in social security benefits, faster than industrial output and faster than retail prices. So Britain has often been first in the rise of the rate of inflation. The £1 that was decimalized in 1971 was worth 28p ten years later.

Britain, even when it has not been first, has never been far behind in the expansion of the public service sector of the economy, either financed directly by taxes or by charges (as with electricity, gas and the post office) that are often manipulated as if they were taxes. This has been encouraged as much by Conservative as by Labour governments. Wherever it has meant loss of productiveness by industry and over-manning in central and local government, Britain has been among the first to be overburdened by bureaucracy.

So it is not surprising that Britain's share of world trade has been falling fairly consistently; it probably should be a surprise for our critics that Britain is still the fifth largest trader in the world and that, in exporting a quarter of everything we make and do, we outclass all our main rivals.

And although Britain is certainly not the first, not even in western Europe, to develop a cash-only, or black, economy, it may be seen as a sign of a native ingenuity as much as our national dishonesty that it is at least growing. If the Inland Revenue puts it at 7.5 per cent of the official gross national product, it is very likely to be much more.

It means, simply, that many of us have found our own answer to high taxes, overmanning and unemployment and are doing more hard work—at goods and services the customers really want—than we are prepared to admit. We are doing the taxman down, of course, but it would be nice to think that one reason is our decent reluctance to deprive the world of its simple pleasure in saying what a lazy lot we are. That, too, is a role of sorts.

In all this the plain people have made their way as best they could. We have taken the prosperity of the post-war world—modest though some of Britain's prosperity has been compared with other people's—and we show every sign of meaning to hold on to what we have got in the new, post-Keynesian era.

Though the diminution of class consciousness is heatedly denied by reformers, and racial distrust is probably increasing, most of us lead quietly reassuring lives, surrounded by expensive possessions and travelling as never before. If we are preoccupied by anything it is by entertainment and leisure. In the quarter of a century between 1950 and 1974 real incomes doubled.

Women have insisted on greater equality with men, especially in earnings. They have not always got it, not by any means, and the stridency of some has helped to consolidate the obduracy of partly-frightened males. But more and more married women have gone out to work to keep up family income and increase family belongings. Although this may not have helped to improve family cohesion or the children's sense of discipline and security, work has been the great liberator. When the economy is expanding, it seems that nearly one woman in two has a job of some sort, often part-time. This is much higher than in western Europe.

Contraception has been the other liberator. More and more women, both married and single, have taken to the pill and other anti-pregnancy devices. Not all have become happier or healthier, but the revolution will not be turned back now. Abortion has been legalized and that, too, is not likely to change. This freedom from sexual worries has prompted a frankness about sexual behaviour that would have startled other generations. For some young people the price of promiscuity and pornography may prove high.

Still, the opportunities for British hypocrisy remain undiminished. Middle-class morality professed to be outraged when it heard in 1963 that the secretary for war, the unfortunate John Profumo, had been caught sleeping around; rumours of other ministers' cavortings abounded. Even in 1973, two ministers had to resign when they were caught. Nor did the 1957 Wolfenden report and the alleviation of the law on adult homosexuality save Jeremy Thorpe from a torrent of innuendo long before he came to stand trial, charged with conspiracy to murder, in 1979. Our love of scandal seems undimmed.

We have arranged our tax and subsidy

systems to give the highest encouragement to housing. This has distorted investment, but it has produced results. The population has risen by over five million (ten per cent) since the war; families are smaller; households have nearly doubled. After the war most people still rented their homes from private owners. Yet now more than half own their own homes, and most of the others are in council estates and tower blocks.

More than half the homes have full or partial central heating; the coal fire burning in the grate has become a rarity.

Our possessions have multiplied. After the war only one-third of families had a car; now the figure is approaching two-thirds. And more than a tenth of families has more than one. Homes with television sets rose from almost none to almost all in 20 years; well over half the sets are now colour.

In the same time cinema audiences, despite all sorts of innovations, have inevitably fallen—from nearly half the population going off to the local fleapit twice a week in the 1940s to just one in ten going once a month in the 1970s. People now read more books, buying them or borrowing them from public libraries, and fewer newspapers.

Homes with a telephone have risen from just 1.5 million to nearly 12 million—which still leaves some nine million, chiefly working-class, homes without one and at the mercy of the local phone-box vandals. The British dislike of the telephone may be psychological; or it may be that it is usually difficult to get one, as it is the only gadget that must both be ordered from, and installed by, a nationalized corporation.

Nearly all homes have a refrigerator; three-quarters of them have a washing machine; two-fifths have a deep freeze. This has not turned the proletariat into a bourgeoisie. Nor, apart from home ownership, has it changed voting habits appreciably. But, even at times of high and rising unemployment, it means Britain is another country from the one that survived the 1930s.

As we have grown richer and fatter, we have eaten less bread and potatoes than our parents did. When meat rationing ended

(as late as 1956) we promptly began to eat much more meat than our parents did. We now eat eight times as much poultry as before. The broiler chicken has replaced the roast beef of old England as the national delicacy.

And, of course, taste is much more cosmopolitan. More than a quarter of family spending on food goes on convenience foods: not just the old fish and chips, but take-away curry, chop-suey, kebabs and hamburgers. The old teashops have mostly gone.

This prosperity has driven us to drink more: more, that is, of everything alcoholic. At home we are drinking less tea and more coffee. And many of us, especially in the middle class, are stopping smoking. In the 1950s we spent more on tobacco than we did on alcohol; now we spend less. This is a health campaign that has worked up to a point. The tax on cigarettes is becoming, almost exclusively, a tax on working-class men—and women.

We spend more on clothes and dress more informally, perhaps more democratically. The bowler hat has gone out; jeans have come in, and have come in to stay. Skirts have gone from the midi (the New Look of the late 1940s) to the mini, to the maxi, and to the midi again; the fashions changed nearly as quickly as economic policies.

Even women who did not follow Mary Quant had their sense of style revolutionized by Marks and Spencer. The coming of tights sent panic through the hosiery industry. Men, too, have become much less conservative: their trousers have gone all the way from drainpipes to flares—except, of course, at Royal Ascot.

For a people said to take their pleasures sadly and sparingly, we have begun to branch out. The old-fashioned, taciturn sports fans going out in cloth caps in all weathers to watch soccer, horse-racing and cricket have found something else to do. Attendances at these three national pastimes have halved (from 78 million a year in 1951 to 36 million in 1976). Some of the one-time spectators are now helping with the Saturday shopping. Many soccer fans were scared away by the hooligans. Cricket, under Kerry Packer and Tony Greig, has become wholly commercial; the three-day county game is almost dead. But swimming, golf and squash are on the up and up. So, still, is jogging. And television has made new sports for the millions, such as tennis and show-jumping, and has even revived snooker and darts.

We all gamble more: from casinos in London's West End to bingo halls and betting shops. Over a third of all adults do the pools.

And we have been given, and have taken, more holidays. By 1961 manual workers had only two weeks a year; by 1977 they all had three weeks and a third of them had four. We have taken our holidays away from home and away from relatives' homes, too. Blackpool survived, but the caravan parks have spread round the coasts and up into the hills.

Those going on package holidays abroad doubled. They mostly still go to Spain but now some even go to America—since Freddie Laker went to court to beat the Labour government and British Airways.

And we have changed the very face of the land, as it had not been changed for generations. Council estates, middle-class suburbia, asphalt, brick and concrete have spread out from the cities and towns. New towns, 32 of them, have grown up in what were green fields. Over 1,500 miles of motorway traverse the country. The great estuaries have been bridged or tunnelled. Coniferous forests march up the mountainsides, so that nearly a tenth of the land has been taken over by trees.

The rolling English countryside, set with

Picketers' paradise. The big steel strike, the first since 1926, that began in January 1980 was fought between a government that denied it could do anything and flying pickets who tried to stop all private steel producers, especially (below) Hadfields in Sheffield. Within months several nationalized plants were shut for good, and Hadfields were making bad losses.

hedges, streams and meadows, has been torn apart. A quarter of the hedgerows have gone, and with them their wild flowers; streams are deepened into drainage channels, the meadows put down to rye grass, the plough drives industriously over down and moor. When the spring winds blow over the fens, dust clouds rise. The very cattle in the fields are increasingly of European breeds. By these means we now grow over half our food.

Perhaps the highest penalty paid for the years of economic ill-success has been a steadily pervading cynicism: a sense that the political system could not be made to work; that its institutions and manners, having served their day, had become merely a frontage for failure; that the United Kingdom itself might be on the point of coming apart at the seams.

In politics this mood has prompted ever more extreme solutions to be propagated on both left and right, while the undogmatic middle has muttered about centre parties, social democracy, bills of rights, and even a businesslike coalition to run Great Britain Ltd. It all encouraged the various Liberal revivals, especially in the winter of 1973–74, and the Social Democrats of 1981.

In Scotland and Wales, however, it became more serious earlier, and for more compelling reasons. Each country retained a stronger feeling of its own national identity than the English, increasingly by far the biggest and richest nation on the island, ever chose to understand. Both Scots and Welsh knew that when prosperity touched them it was a briefer and thinner prosperity than almost anywhere else in western Europe, and so they looked especially dubiously at the very idea of the Common Market.

Then suddenly, by the early 1970s the first exploitation of North Sea oil gave the Scottish Nationalists a credible economic policy and a slogan: it was Scotland's oil. By October 1974, they had won 11 seats in the Commons and were the second party in 42 others.

The unionist parties' reply to this was confused, divided and often incompetent, but it worked. The Scots and Welsh were given a referendum each on a form of self-government that would come about only if 40 per cent of their total electorates voted Yes. The Welsh, divided by their language, voted No anyway. In Scotland, though 52 per cent of those who voted said Yes, that was only 33 per cent of the electorate.

That was devolution, that was. To some the whole referendum idea was a cheat, to others a sensible device that had claims to be regarded as one of the better, if unsung, aspects of Labour's political management in the decade.

That it was the Scottish Nationalists' resentment at being out-manoeuvred which helped decisively to bring down the Callaghan government in the vote of no confidence in March 1979, and which in turn precipitated the Nationalists' own defeat in the general election, was in itself a parable of the sourness that might have broken up the kingdom—and may still do so one day.

The malignity in Northern Ireland from 1969 onwards took the British largely unawares, and we had no crisis management to cope with it. Having tacitly supported the Protestant ascendancy since partition, and taking care only not to ask questions about it, the politicians and civil servants in London were surprised to find both that the Catholic minority wanted civil rights, especially in housing and employment, beyond the freedom of worship and education they enjoyed, and that the most liberal of the Protestants, Terence O'Neill, could not persuade enough of the majority to concede such rights.

For a brief time the British believed in miracles. We thought disarming all the police would bring peace. We thought the army could be accepted as neutral. We thought Bernadette Devlin, elected to the Commons at Westminster in April 1969, was just a young civil rights campaigner, and that the Reverend Ian Paisley, who arrived there a year later, was too much of a zealot ever to be taken seriously.

Later, the authorities were to believe variously that a show of force—'Bloody Sunday' in Londonderry in January 1972, when 13 Catholics were shot dead—would calm things, or that abolishing the Stormont parliament would do it, or that a power-sharing executive and an assembly based on proportional representation would.

Nothing did. Over 2,000 people have died in Northern Ireland, among them more than 500 from the security forces. Over 22,000 have been injured.

Most British politicians, having believed it their responsibility not to rule the six counties themselves, now seem to believe that direct rule there is the lesser evil for Ireland, and assume that governments in the south can be persuaded to accept it.

It has meant accepting a lengthy army casualty list, bombs in London and Birmingham as well as Belfast, the expenditure of hundreds of millions of pounds, and the arrival of more Northern Ireland MPs at Westminster. It is not that most of the British would have minded if the province had detached itself. But we probably would have minded if the detachment had meant even more bloodshed. In a way, it has been a dilemma; but in a way it has been a role.

More than any of her subjects, the Queen has had a role, knew it, and did it well. As Britain's reputation in the world has diminished, the reputation of the monarchy has grown, much to republican distress.

The Queen's silver jubilee progress was a spectacular success, and the celebrations were most enjoyed and most spontaneous in working-class districts; but it had not been easily won in the 25 years beforehand. Her father, a shy and good man, had restored respect for the monarchy, but the extravagant forecasts of a new Elizabethan age that greeted her accession in 1952 did her no favours.

Diligently, she set an example for the virtues of family life and was soon told that her voice and ideals were 'frankly a pain in the neck' (Lord Altrincham) and her person 'dowdy, frumpy and banal' (Malcolm Muggeridge). Indiscretions in the family, especially those of Princess Margaret and Princess Anne, have been relentlessly reported. No increase in the civil list passes without criticism. Yet she has won through, a symbol of more than national continuity and common sense.

Her reminder to Parliament in Westminster Hall in 1977 that she could not

Rummy's record. Steeplechasing in the 1970s
was dominated by Red Rum
(here with Brian Fletcher up), the first horse
ever to win the Grand National three times.
He did it in 1973 (9–1), 1974 (11–1)
and 1977 (9–1). Then he retired to carry out such
public engagements as opening supermarkets
and switching on Blackpool's lights.
He'd probably have made speeches too,
if he'd been asked.

forget she had been crowned queen of a United Kingdom was much more than a casual remark in the era of devolution; her presence at the Commonwealth conference at Lusaka in 1979 contributed to the adaptation of British policy on Rhodesia. As the years have passed she has become the government official who has read more state papers than any other, has had more experience of foreign governments than her diplomats, and has more inside knowledge of the process of governing than any of her prime ministers.

Her only remaining power is the power to give advice. She has not diminished it. And if public affection is the popular test for monarchy in a television age she now passes it effortlessly.

What no one guessed, as Britain picked itself up after the war, was that so much energy, devotion and imagination would go into the arts as they had never gone before, even when the country had been at its most prosperous. It may have been because we were anxious about ourselves, that for once we needed to know what was happening to us and what might happen, and so turned especially to the new people in the theatre, in the novel and in painting to tell us.

Many of these new people turned out to be obsessed with class; this obsession made their work less interesting but most successful as entertainment. The other obsession was with sex, invariably with the same success. Sometimes their rebellion blew out into the gentlest of conventional zephyrs. Sometimes it ended in absurdity and eccentricity. But they gave the country a run for the taxpayers' money.

In the theatre the heroic style did not long survive the memories of the war; and the great men, Olivier, Richardson and Gielgud, had to adapt to the times. Olivier adapted most successfully. He began the 35 years being knighted and ended being elected to the Order of Merit. The 'thirties style, epitomized by Noel Coward, was not adaptable. What the audiences lapped up were the angry young men from the provinces, redbrick-educated, uncertain, insecure, committed only to their diatribe against society.

It began with John Osborne's Jimmy Porter in *Look Back in Anger*, appropriately in 1956, the year of the invasions of Suez and Hungary. Osborne struck again with *The Entertainer* next year, enlisting Olivier to condemn Britain through the mouth of a shabby music-hall comedian.

This was the way to get at Harold Macmillan and the bourgeoisie, and a host of talent was ready to oblige. Arnold Wesker, Shelagh Delaney, and Keith Waterhouse and Willis Hall put the working-class ethos to work. Harold Pinter preferred the comedy of menace, Joe Orton just to shock. Satire, nourished by the BBC's *That Was The Week That Was*, was all the rage.

London's 40 theatres had great names on stage: Guinness, Scofield, Evans, Ashcroft, Finney, Jackson, Redgrave. And they were packed to the doors. Ten years after, when the economy was faltering, the wave of protest had spent itself. The West End stage seemed back to mild irreverence (Tom Stoppard) or just poking fun at the new middle class (Alan Ayckbourn and Alan Bennett). The recession proper meant dark theatres—or big musical revivals.

Much of the success sprang from George

Devine's English Stage Company, which used its financial windfalls to engage in new experiments. But at the theatre's height there was a luxury of choice. Joan Littlewood, with her Theatre Workshop in the East End, and Bernard Miles, with his Mermaid, were in the forefront too. The fringe thrived and spread.

So, too, did the official theatre. The Arts Council began in a small way in 1946: its first grant from the Treasury was just £235,000 (now it gets £80 million a year). Its money helped, but it also helped politically. The National Theatre Company opened at the Old Vic in 1963, with Olivier as its first artistic director and Kenneth Tynan his literary adviser. Eventually, the National got its own building on the South Bank—and the Old Vic was told to close.

The Royal Shakespeare Company, driven on and up by Peter Hall, was already in place to challenge the National from Stratford and the Aldwych. Between them they gave astonishing life to the classical repertoire. London's international reputation, and the tourist industry, soared.

For the tourists there were, of course, other delights as well. British farce flourished at the Whitehall. Nudity, after the closure of the genteel Revudeville at the Windmill in 1964, flourished almost everywhere. The cult of *The Mousetrap* has kept actors in work and management in funds from 1952 to (it seems) doomsday. And in Tim Rice and Andrew Lloyd Webber London even had a winning team for hit musicals, *Jesus Christ Superstar* and *Evita*.

The novelists, too, helped to perpetuate class-consciousness, though usually in a more disparate and picaresque way. The generation of Evelyn Waugh, Rebecca West and Graham Greene gave in to the young and disillusioned, whose anti-heroes, besides being dissatisfied with their birth and education, invariably wished to escape from the rigours of provincial life. This was the formula of Kingsley Amis, John Braine, William Cooper and Alan Sillitoe. It was also, in a tragic way, what happened to the Welsh poet, Dylan Thomas (*Under Milk Wood*).

It seemed a trifle hard on the provinces that, flattered by the attention of being

The way to go.
Victor the giraffe at Marwell Zoological Park, Winchester, collapsed entirely in September 1977 and, anxiously though the country waited for better news, not even lifting tackle ever got him back on his feet again.
It seemed he had selflessly made three female giraffes happy on his last, active night.

written about again, it was mainly as places from which the upwardly-mobile went to London and the south-east. Only there, in real life, was it a mark of success to have a provincial accent.

Women, the depressed sex, were well catered for by Margaret Drabble and Edna O'Brien (born in Co. Clare), and in a sprightlier fashion by Muriel Spark. But overhanging all these domestic matters was the symbolism of George Orwell. He died all too soon after the war, but the relevance of the politics of *Animal Farm* and, even more, the totalitarian society of *1984* (written in 1948) continued ominously through the second half of the century and, perhaps more than any other work from the elite, influenced plain people's thoughts.

The British cinema had virtually dropped out by the 1970s. It had long had a hard fight financially, and once the easy postwar days were over its best people needed to move into international co-production or abroad to stay at work. Its most memorable style was that of the Ealing comedies, nicely-observed but undemanding scenes of eccentric British life, most memorably *The*

Lavender Hill Mob, Passport to Pimlico, and *Whisky Galore*. They explored, tolerantly, these backwaters before they disappeared in a harsher current.

The Boulting brothers were satirical about conscription in *Private's Progress*, redbrick universities in *Lucky Jim* and, most tellingly, trade unions in *I'm All Right, Jack*, with Peter Sellers. The cinema's rediscovery of northern England was chiefly derivative, relying on the novels of Braine (*Room at the Top*), Stan Barstow (*A Kind of Loving*) and David Storey (*This Sporting Life*). In the late 1960s and early 1970s television inspired new directors ranging from realism to fantasy in John Schlesinger, Kenneth Loach and Ken Russell.

Painting had its kitchen-sink days with John Bratby in the 1950s, but that was promptly and almost brusquely pushed aside by the arrival of pop. This British pop style was American-inspired, but it was given a distinctiveness by the Independent Group, and especially Richard Hamilton.

The *This Is Tomorrow* exhibition at Whitechapel in 1956 took up the running in gimmickry, glamour, popularity, wit and success, and this was continued, partly under the aegis of Richard Smith, with the *Young Contemporaries* exhibition in 1961. This produced two names that even the unsuspecting public came to hear of: David Hockney and Allen Jones.

Hockney broke out of Bradford straight into the limelight, almost as if he were a blond Beatle with stunningly precocious gifts. The critics have become less rapturous about him and Jones now. But these years put an energy and a directness into British painting which gave excitement to what painting was saying, whatever that was.

Much less was heard and made of the internationally-recognized painter, Francis Bacon (born in Dublin). But his human figures, often caught in isolation and violence, seemed characteristic of the age, and of an artist engaged in an assault on the nervous system.

To the popular media, almost unaware of what was happening in art, the chief centre of controversy happened to be Graham Sutherland who, while moving serenely from landscape deeper into symbolism, took two commissions. In one he perpetrated an unconventional tapestry for the new Coventry cathedral; in the other a less-than-flattering presentation portrait of Winston Churchill. The tapestry was decried; the painting was burned by Lady Churchill.

In sculpture Henry Moore had too high an international reputation, and had been around too long (since the 1930s), for there to be any controversy about him. Barbara Hepworth and Anthony Caro managed some, but the full quota of unthinking wrath was directed at Reg Butler, whose *Unknown Political Prisoner* had actually been awarded a prize.

Whatever the artist's feelings, there was much fun to be had in this way, and was had by all. If the Tate gallery bought a pile of bricks or a nude arrived in a wheelbarrow at the Edinburgh festival, outrage became an art form in itself.

And music came into its own. Vaughan Williams was still composing major works until his death in 1958, and Havergal Brian composed the majority of his symphonies after the war. But there was a new audience, and new ideas.

Benjamin Britten at Aldeburgh was prolific and deservedly popular. And other new men, often products of the Royal Academy of Music and the Royal College of Music, were pressing forward: Edmund Rubbra, a pupil of Holst; Michael Tippett, relishing his revolutionary reputation; Malcolm Arnold and Iain Hamilton. To some concert-goers, the younger generation of Peter Maxwell Davies and Richard Rodney Bennett has been even more interesting.

The Royal Festival Hall was built. The great orchestras, in London and the provinces, won new reputations, recording contracts and foreign tours. Perhaps the greatest achievement of all was the BBC's popularization of classical—and modern—music through all the post-war decades. The promenade concerts at the Albert Hall were a perennial success, but beyond that the BBC's orchestras employed for most of the time one-third of the country's full-time professional musicians—an unparalleled contribution. There were 90 hours of music a week on BBC Radio 3.

Outside London, festivals have thrived. The Edinburgh International Festival has built up an international following. Cheltenham has concentrated on contemporary British music. Up and down the country every taste has had its solace, from the Three Choirs in West Country cathedrals to the Gaelic Mod and the Royal National Eisteddfod.

Opera, heavily subsidized, has flourished for its devotees at Covent Garden, Sadler's Wells and the summer lawns of Glyndebourne.

The Royal Ballet produced international stars in Margot Fonteyn, Beryl Grey, Robert Helpmann and—the Russian émigré who chose Covent Garden in 1962—Rudolf Nureyev. Yet the ascendancy of British ballet owes as much to an unrivalled group of choreographers: Ninette de Valois, Frederick Ashton, Kenneth MacMillan and John Cranko.

British pop music carried all before it in the generation of the Beatles, the Rolling Stones, the Bay City Rollers, the Who, Cream, Pink Floyd and innumerable others. Then there was punk. It is not finished yet, not by any means, this fullness, this plenitude of young musicians and singers, the voices of their age, who have become household names around the world.

These were the years when we got used to worrying about ourselves. We were encouraged in this by the plethora of advisers and critics who descended on us to prove their own predilections, from the ruin of capitalism to the emergence of the first post-industrial state.

It seems wisest now to remember that Britain is still a pleasant enough place to live: one which does not exist in awe of an oppressive neighbour; where people can still say what they think; where the poor, the old and the young are better off than they were half a lifetime ago; and where milk bottles and weather arrive without fail on the doorstep every morning.

Like any generation, ours has inherited problems and worries and will pass them on. They are far from unique. We have tried to do too much, no doubt, and we have expected too much; and we have chopped and changed our ideas and our remedies too often. But we have put our energy into successes too.

No, they have not been the best of years for us; but not quite the worst.

Royal permission. The Queen, after taking the Privy Council's advice,
gave her formal approval to the marriage of the Prince of Wales
and Lady Diana Spencer at St Paul's Cathedral
(bigger than Westminster Abbey) on 29 July 1981.
The nation settled down to a day in front of the telly.

Who won the war anyway?

The Britain that came out of the war in Europe on 8 May 1945 (and out of the war against Japan on 2 September) was battered and shabby, cocky and hopeful. Montgomery took one surrender at Luneberg Heath, Mountbatten the other at Singapore. After six years and 400,000 dead, 61,000 of them civilians, church bells rang and the lights came on again. Half a million homes lay in ruins. But it had been the war to end wars. It was time for a new start.

There was, almost at once, a new Labour government. The general election was on 5 July and, when the votes were counted on 26 July (to allow the Service vote to be flown home), Labour had triumphed. Although Churchill drew enormous crowds in the campaign, they represented gratitude for victory not support for the future and he was beaten by 15 million votes to 10 million. When his wife suggested defeat might be a blessing in disguise, Churchill replied that he found it 'most effectively disguised'.

Attlee, the winner, refused to wait to be re-elected party leader and drove straight to the Palace to kiss hands. He was brisk, businesslike, a man of few words. Before the election Churchill had taken him to meet Truman and Stalin at the Potsdam summit: now Attlee returned alone. He no more trusted Stalin than Churchill had done and his policy of building the West's defences in Europe had backing from the Tories, though not from Labour's left wing.

Attlee was determined to give India its independence: the last viceroy, Mountbatten, did this in August 1947 even though it meant partition with Pakistan, chaos, killings and millions homeless. Under American pressure and Zionist guerrilla attacks, Attlee also accepted the inevitable in Palestine and ended the mandate in 1948.

In the bright morning of the 1945 election few expectations were too high for the first majority Labour government to entertain. Nationalization was pushed through: starting with the Bank of England (for cosmetic reasons), followed by the coal industry, civil aviation, electricity, railways and long-distance road transport. It seemed revolutionary but had all been long planned. Four-fifths of the country's workers still had private employers.

Next came the redemption of Labour's other promises in the 1930s: social insurance, family allowances, national assistance (successor to the dole) and, above all,

the National Health Service. From July 1948, this eagerly adopted child of Nye Bevan became a beacon light for the whole welfare state. No one alive before the Health Service could have absolutely any doubt about the change it made in British life and expectations.

Yet, in a very short time, Labour seemed to be struggling. Britain was hugely in debt because of the war. Industry was clapped-out. The winter of 1946–47 was the worst of the century; coal and electricity simply ran out. The economic loan from America soon threatened to run out, too, just through keeping Britain fed.

The depressing predicament of low productivity, inadequate exports and a growing payments deficit overtook the Attlee government while it was still in the first enthusiasm of its socialist programme. Its remedies, like the predicament, were to be repeated frequently, though not always so drastically.

There was austerity: tighter rationing, a capital levy, a new economic plan, exhortation to exporters and, finally, the £1 was devalued from $4.03 to $2.80. Exports, indeed, occasionally responded and Marshall aid helped recovery. Yet the trade account was vulnerable to even a minor American recession, or a dock strike, and the government grew rattled.

On to 1984. George Orwell (real name Eric Blair) looked at the collectivist post-war future and decided he did not fancy it one bit. His satire was astringent and timely.

The faces of victory. The big three met for the last time at Yalta, on the Crimean coast, in February 1945. Churchill was unhappy that he could not stop the Soviets taking over Poland, for whose independence Britain had gone to war. But Roosevelt, deteriorating before their eyes, sided with Stalin, and Stalin was adamant. Two months later FDR was dead.

Shinwell declared that anyone who was not an organized worker did 'not matter a tinker's curse' and Bevan called the Tories 'lower than vermin'. Such statements merely hid the truth that the government was divided and that its self-confidence was ebbing away.

Breakup was steady. Dalton, confessing to a minor budget leak, went in 1947. Bevin died and Morrison, his successor as foreign secretary, was a flop when the Shah and Dr Mossadeq nationalized the Anglo-Iranian oil company. Cripps became seriously ill and gave way to Gaitskell. It even seemed, after Attlee scraped back in the 1950 election with a majority of six, that Labour had exhausted the very ideas and ambitions that had brought it to power. Rearmament and the Korean war speeded up the Bevanite revolt. In October 1951 the government succumbed.

Still, it was not all plain living. Much ceremonial was dusted off for the first time when Princess Elizabeth married Prince Philip in November 1947. The Festival of Britain tried to uplift and entertain in the summer of 1951, though it was not a critical success. The Royal Opera House reopened in 1946 (it had been a dance hall in the war) with Frederick Ashton and David Webster in charge. In 1947 the Edinburgh festival made its bow.

And, in 1948, the New Look arrived from Paris. It took over fashion so quickly and completely that there was soon a glut of the old utility styles and the authorities had to relax the clothing ration. This particular lesson was not lost on Harold Wilson, the century's youngest cabinet member and President of the Board of Trade, who took to announcing his 'bonfire of controls'.

Sport, too, was back—though Britain did not exactly shine. Bradman and the Australians came and gave England a nostalgic thrashing. The Olympics came to London. Then, in 1950, the West Indies came and Ramadhin and Valentine won three of the four Tests; French horses won four of the five classics; and the BRM, the new racing car, drove into fiasco.

On 25 May 1951, two diplomats absconded. They were Burgess and Maclean. Six years after the British had won the war, no one doubted—at least not in Fleet Street—that the Cold War was on.

We shall have MOUSSEC wherever we go
LONDON HIPPODROME
IVOR NOVELLO
Perchance to Dream
RANDALLS
PUBLIC
SHELTER

Victory in Europe was declared on 8 May 1945.
The crowds filled Trafalgar Square (preceding pages),
stopping the traffic and prompting Alanbrooke,
chief of the imperial general staff, to say,
'A day disorganized by victory.
A form of disorganization I can put up with'.
Churchill emerged from Downing Street
into Whitehall and was promptly mobbed.
He insisted on driving to Buckingham Palace
in an open car, arrived late and then appeared
on the balcony with the royal family (above).
The King told him, 'Five years ago you told us
we would get nothing but blood,
sweat and tears . . . I should say that is
a fair estimate of what we did get'.
London, and especially the American forces,
duly got lit up when the lights went on again (above)
and even the royal princesses were allowed out,
for the first time, to join the crowds.
Halfway across Europe, Montgomery had read
the surrender terms to the German military (right)
at his Luneberg Heath headquarters.

Churchill wanted to go on
until the Japanese surrendered,
but Labour insisted on an early general election.
So, it was only as a caretaker prime minister
that Churchill went off to meet Truman (below)
and Stalin at the Potsdam conference.
He was gloomy about giving up
so much of central Europe to the Soviet Union,
and grieved that British power
had diminished 'in this gaunt world'.
In the election the Service vote (above)
may have made all the difference;
it was estimated that nine-tenths
of it went to Labour.
While the Conservatives relied on Churchill and the call
'Help Him Finish the Job',
Labour had the greater appeal (top right)
on jobs, housing and health.
When the Labour sweep was known
on 26 July, Clem Attlee and his wife
went to Transport House (bottom right)
and that evening Mrs Attlee
drove him to the Palace
in their small Austin car
to kiss hands and form a government.

The King and Queen toured the country
to celebrate and commiserate.
The Queen was popular in the East End
of London (above left). She had said,
when Buckingham Palace was bombed,
'I'm glad we've been bombed.
It means I can look
the East End in the face'.
The United Nations charter was drafted
to bring order to the world.
Amid qualms about Soviet ambitions Halifax,
the British ambassador (above),
signed in San Francisco in June 1945.
The Services were demob-happy.
They grumbled at delays, but usually

cheered up on drawing their first
civvy suit (top right-centre); then
out into the world of clothing coupons.
In their best suits the senior men
of the new Labour government (top right)
posed for their picture with the King.
Left to right: Morrison,
Attlee, Greenwood, Bevin, Alexander.
The King got on well with them.
He particularly liked Bevin,
the foreign secretary.
The hard-headed Vyacheslav Molotov
(above) was Stalin's mouthpiece and
negotiator with the West through seemingly
interminable conferences that merely

increased the divisions and suspicions
of the immediate post-war world.
The Cold War was beginning.
The British economy was so parlous,
especially after the abrupt ending
of lend-lease, that the Attlee government
had to turn to the United States for aid.
The economist, Maynard Keynes (below far left),
was sent to negotiate a loan
of $3,750 million,
at two per cent interest, in 1945.
Canada lent $1,250 million.
Keynes called it 'an act
of unprecedented liberality',
but the money soon drained away

just keeping the country fed;
it was not until Marshall aid
began in 1947 that Bevin felt able to say,
'Britain has been reborn'.
At Nuremberg (above) the allies met,
with legal dignity, to unfold the story
of German war crimes and to judge
the surviving Nazi leaders, chiefly
Goering (leaning on elbow), Hess
and Ribbentrop. Ribbentrop was hanged
and Goering took cyanide in his cell.
Hess endured, the solitary prisoner of Spandau.
The arts recovered and theatres were full:
Richardson and Olivier (above centre)
starred in *Uncle Vanya*.

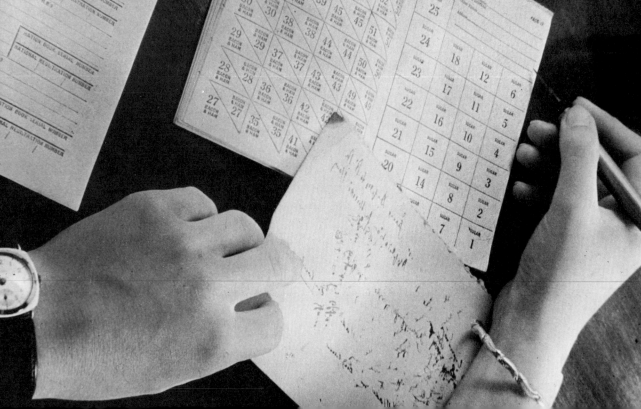

Out of power, Churchill ruminated on the world scene
both in his speeches warning, as at Fulton,
against Soviet designs and in his own history of the war.
He left to others, chiefly Rab Butler,
the task of modernizing the Conservative party
and its policies. And at Miami (left), the south of France
and anywhere he could set up an easel, he painted.
For the Labour government, the difficulties grew.
Everything, it seemed, was scarce: socialism
and austerity came to be synonymous.
Housewives were hard put to eke out the bacon
and ham and sugar (below left) in their ration books.
Even bread was rationed.
Housing was dilapidated. In the big cities
like Liverpool (right) what the bombs had spared
was often not worth sparing, except that families
had nowhere else to go. The government's reputation
was soured, and the Conservatives
began to promise priority for new housing.
Try as it did to find anything edible
to put on the shop shelves, the Ministry of Food
knew no limits in its searches. Snoek (below),
a fish resembling the barracuda, was strongly promoted
in 1947–48 and even made to look appetizing on the tin.
But unlike such delicacies as spam,
dried egg and even dried banana, it never caught on.
Whalemeat had its fanciers and in texture,
if not in taste, was preferable to horsemeat.
An ominous newspaper heading about one food minister,
'Webb to be pressed for more sausages',

proved an exaggeration.
Labour eagerly agreed to implement
the Education Act of 1944 which had been passed
by the wartime coalition. It provided,
for the first time, secondary education
for all children. This meant a division,
settled by the 11-plus examination,
between children going to grammar schools,
technical schools or just secondary modern schools.
Everyone thought it a great step forward
until middle-class children began failing the 11-plus.
The public schools, like Eton (above right),
were unchanged and, indeed, unchallenged,
despite the hopeful claims that they were
being overtaken by the grammar schools
which, had they known it,
were to be the more threatened species.

The Labour government had little luck.
The winter of 1946–47 was appalling, probably
the worst since 1880. The country was chilled
to the marrow. Electricity was cut,
so that lanterns (below right) had to come out of store.
What was worse, blizzards blocked the railways
(right) so that coal could not be moved from the pits.
This was a particularly poor start
for the new National Coal Board
which took over on 1 January 1947.
The fuel minister, Shinwell, a likeable man
of greater volubility than talent,
had to cut back power for industry,
making 4.5 million unemployed,
and cut off homes altogether mornings and afternoons.
The winter dragged on until April.
The government called on private enthusiasm
to go to the railway sidings and unload
any coal wagons that could be found.
There was a response:
the wartime spirit had not gone yet.
But the fuel crisis helped
to emphasize Labour's sense of failure.
Nationalization, too, from the moment it began,
was dogged by disappointment.
Within a year the new fuel minister, Gaitskell,
had to confess about nationalizing coal,
'We thought we knew all about it;
but the matter of fact was we did not'.
Productivity stayed dishearteningly down,
which handicapped industry and the exports drive.
For the miners themselves the new managers
were frustratingly like the old ones.
The queue became a national habit. When word
reached the housewives of Islington that potatoes were
to be had at Mr Harris's fruit and vegetable shop
in the Essex Road, 1,000 turned up to try their luck.
It was a big enough queue
for even the law to take an interest.

India's hour had come. From the moment Attlee despatched the new (and last) viceroy, Lord Mountbatten, and his wife Edwina (seen with Gandhi, right), Britain was determined to grant independence, whatever the cost or complications. The cost was high in lives as Hindu and Moslem fought each other; the chief complication was partition, leaving India and Pakistan unstable rivals on the sub-continent, but both stayed in the Commonwealth. Mountbatten was much admired, often justly, for his drive, his tact and his ability to win the trust of all sides. He and his wife were there in Government House, New Delhi (below), when Jawaharlal Nehru's new cabinet was sworn in, including the one woman, Rajkumari Amrit Kaur.

The bright hope of the Attlee government
was Harold Wilson, promoted to succeed
Cripps at the Board of Trade
in September 1947. He was, at 31,
the youngest cabinet minister
since Pitt and his mother (left)
was naturally proud of him. He worked
hard on his working-class reputation,
gradually threw off his donnish
and civil-service reticence
and began, modestly, to set fire
to some socialist restrictions.
This was as well, for the New Look,
arriving from Paris (below),
played havoc with long-inculcated
notions of austerity and utility.
A little glamour,
a little style,
was what was wanted,
whatever the ration books said.

Princess Elizabeth was married
on 20 November 1947, at Westminster Abbey,
to Lieutenant Philip Mountbatten, RN.
His title was immediately improved to a dukedom.
It was said to be one of the biggest
royal gatherings of the century
(even including funerals), and it was
a moment for the country to stop worrying
about itself and celebrate.
The bride's gown had been sensibly
supplemented beyond the ration.
They had met in July 1939
when she was taken to Dartmouth by her father;
Philip, a young Greek prince,
had just arrived there.
It was said by her governess
then that Elizabeth 'never took her
eyes off him' and it was,
very plainly, a love match (below)
which greatly pleased her parents
and the country. Even so,
the King made them wait until after
her 21st birthday, and what proved
to be the last royal tour
of South Africa, before agreeing
to the engagement.
Her first son and heir was born
on the evening of Sunday
14 November 1948
at Buckingham Palace where the crowds
had gathered before the news was posted
on the railings. The boy was christened

Charles Philip Arthur George,
and there was much celebration (below)
of one kind and another.
The family moved out to their
own home at Clarence House and,
although there were worries
about the King's health,
the Duke was able to take a posting
as first lieutenant of the destroyer *Chequers*:
his family flew out to Malta to be with him.
On 15 August 1950 a daughter was born,
Anne Elizabeth Alice Louise,
on the same morning as the Duke of Edinburgh
was promoted lieutenant-commander;
his ship was the frigate *Magpie*.
But these days of family life were soon to end.

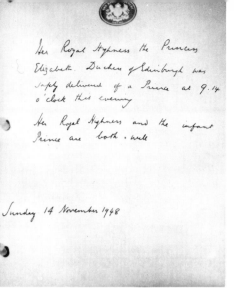

Her Royal Highness the Princess Elizabeth, Duchess of Edinburgh was safely delivered of a Prince at 9.14 o'clock this evening

Her Royal Highness and the infant Prince are both well

Sunday 14 November 1948

The cinema queue had become part of British life;
almost everything brought out the 'full-up' signs.
British productions relied heavily on literary
classics. Alec Guinness (below), one of the younger
school of actors who was to go from strength
to strength in character parts, was a much-admired
Fagin in *Oliver Twist*.
The romantic success of the cinema was
The Red Shoes (below right), filmed at Pinewood Studios
with Moira Shearer, Helpmann and Massine.
It drew on, and helped, popular interest in ballet;
its sets and its story of the tussle between
love and art appealed to a humdrum day.
Even more appealing were the Ealing comedies,
by Michael Balcon and his directors,
such as Henry Cornelius's *Passport to Pimlico*
(right, with Richard Hearne
and Philip Stainton as a policeman).
These gave us the chance to laugh at ourselves,
but respectfully, and in the knowledge
that these times were passing quickly.
The literary lion was T. S. Eliot (centre right),
American-born and Nobel prizewinner
for literature in 1948. He had puzzled the British
with his *Waste Land* as far back as 1922
but now he seemed relevant: *Four Quartets*
became widely quoted, and his plays, *Murder in the Cathedral*
and *The Cocktail Party*, enjoyed a vogue.
Olivier, in *Hamlet* (far right),

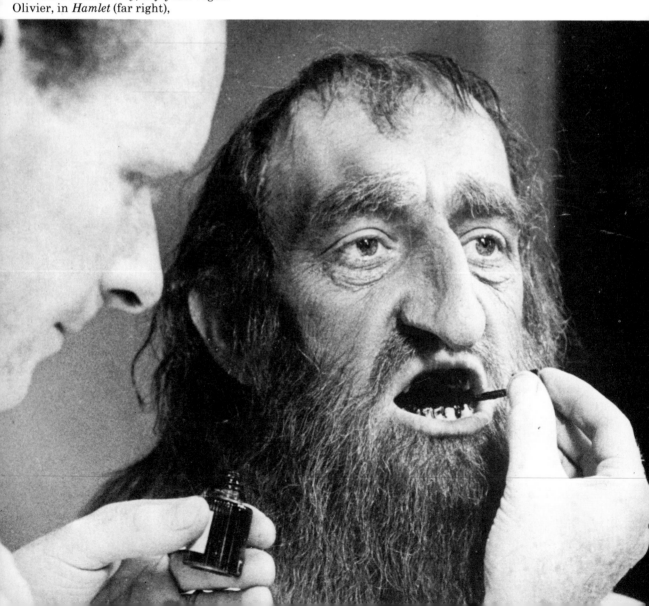

had similar success. These
were for him heroic days,
continuing the fame and prowess
of his roles on
the wartime screen and stage.
New from Nuffield in 1948:
the Morris Minor,
a motor industry success story
which deserved to be a success,
even in a world
short of cheap family cars.
Not so successful, initially,
Britain's new grand-prix racing car,
the BRM (right). But there were
better days ahead.

The sport-starved punters queued
at the turnstiles. In 1948
the Aga Khan (above) led
in his Oaks winner, Masaka (7–1),
ridden by W. Nevett.
He won the Derby with My Love
the same year.
The Aga had been afraid
of German bombs falling on Newmarket
and had sold his best sires,
Blenheim, Bahram and Mahmoud,
to America. But he still had a
great horse to come: Tulyar.
And racing had a new fan:
Princess Elizabeth.
Starting modestly
in National Hunt racing
in joint ownership with her mother,
her royal enthusiasm
was to be rewarded by winning
every classic—except the Derby.
In 1948 the Olympics came to London.
The flame was lit at Wembley
and the British team marched
proudly past (above right)
though only the occasional,
hard-won silver
and bronze medals awaited them.
Germany, Italy and Japan
were not invited.
The Oval Test in 1948 saw the last
appearance of Don Bradman,
the Australian batsman who
had amassed more centuries
against England for more years
than English bowlers
ever care to remember.
Australia had already kept the Ashes
in this series.
For his last innings Bradman was applauded
all the way to the crease (right),
where awaited him, among others,
Hollies (with the ball),
the England captain Yardley
(halfway down the wicket) and
the tall Alec Bedser
(later to be chairman
of the England selectors),
none of whom exactly
fancied his chance
against the great man.
This time Bradman took guard,
faced Hollies,
and was bowled out second ball.
Soccer's crowds returned
in their hundreds of thousands:
too many, sometimes,
for antiquated grounds.
At Burnden Park,
Bolton, in March 1946,
33 fans were killed (left)
at the start of a cup-tie
between Bolton and Stoke
when thousands.
broke down the fencing
and forced their way in.

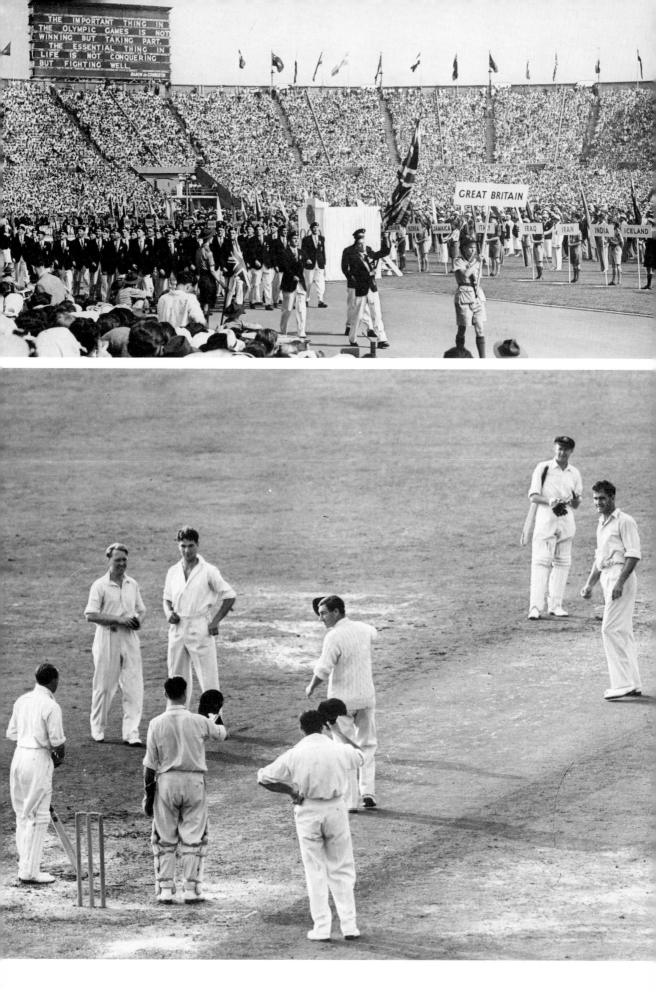

Attlee was not squeamish
about dealing with strikes.
In July 1949, he sent in
the Coldstream and Scots Guards
to unload meat at London docks (left).
Time and again it was
the government's own supporters who failed
to answer appeals to get the country
back in business.
When British Railways were nationalized in 1948
railwaymen wrote, 'This is ours' on their engines.
But neither was that so,
nor did the railways stay
competitive with road transport.
Simply feeding the country was
a recurrent worry.
The land girls (above) were still on the farms,
although modernization was already on the way.
Labour's system of guaranteed prices,
continued from wartime,
began to improve production and farm incomes.

So British farming became a success story.
And there was no talk at all of nationalization.
But the meat ration became a figure of fun.
It was reduced to 8d a week (about 3p)
in April 1949, allowing the alert
Ever-Ready torchmakers a chance
at political advertising (left).
This was all up the Tories' street.
Their chairman, Woolton,
made a point of promising the voters
that they would soon be sinking
their (national health) teeth
into 'good, red meat'.

AH! THERE YOU ARE!

FOUND BY AN

EVER READY
REG'D TRADE MARK

MADE IN BRITAIN

TORCH

The worst moment of Labour's economic manageme
was the devaluation of the £1 from $4.03 to $2.80
on 18 September 1949. Next day the banks and stock
markets were closed, and jobbers (left) had to
mark business out in Throgmorton Street itself.
The rift between Attlee (right) and the more radica
Bevan grew as the government had to cut
back on subsidies and spending.
In February 1950,
Attlee went to the country, campaigning
in his customary unpretentious way.
He got back, but with a majority cut to only six.
He said simply,
'The King's government must be carried on'.
A new generation of youthful Conservatives
picked up seats, especially in suburban England.
One youthful Conservative who failed,
despite enterprising campaigning (below right),
was Margaret Roberts in Dartford.
She got married, had twins,
and reappeared successfully at Finchley,
nine years later,
using her married name, Thatcher.

A tragic embarrassment for Labour
was the failure to hold
Arab and Jew apart in Palestine.
Zionists blew up British headquarters,
the King David Hotel in Jerusalem (above),
killing 90 people.
Britain ended the mandate in May 1948.

The government persisted with the Festival of Britain,
in the summer of 1951, to demonstrate
that a hundred years after the Great Exhibition
Britain was still in the forefront of design and production;
indeed, in everything (left)
from the skylon—virtually unsupported, it was said,
like the economy—to proper chairs.
Queen Mary, touring the festival (below)
with her grandchildren, Prince Michael of Kent (centre)
and Prince William of Gloucester, was not impressed.
She found most of the exhibits
'really extraordinary and very ugly'.
Greater hopes were held of the jet airliner,
the Comet (above), soon to go into service.

The road to Suez

Churchill got back in 1951 even though he had had two strokes and was staring 80 in the face. He won, not because Labour lost support (it received 13,949,000 votes, the highest ever for any party), but because the Liberal vote collapsed his way.

He also got back despite a scare that he was a warmonger. The *Daily Mirror's* front page on election eve demanded, 'Whose finger on the trigger?' But the *Mirror* had got him hopelessly wrong. Churchill was not out to fight the Soviets; at his age what he was looking for was international summitry. 'Talking jaw to jaw,' he told Eisenhower, 'is better than going to war.' Ultimately he even agreed to British withdrawal from the base at Suez. No, it was not Churchill who needed watching; the one they should all have kept their eye on was the irreproachable but nervy Eden, the crown prince.

Churchill did not want to fight anyone at home, either. He allowed Butler, helped by better world trade, to produce expansionary budgets. He denationalized only steel and road transport. He encouraged Macmillan to build over 300,000 houses a year. He stopped food rationing. What was more, he got away with it. The unions did not believe the price index (it was stable) because everyone spent more when rationing ended. But those troubles were for later.

Like Melbourne before him, Churchill had a young Queen to compliment and instruct. The quiet death of George VI in February 1952, while his daughter was asleep at a game reserve in Kenya, put the new Commonwealth into mourning for a decent, dignified man. Queen Elizabeth's coronation in June 1953, on the morning the country heard that a British expedition (actually a New Zealander and a Nepalese) had climbed Everest, was a magnificent show of affection and loyalty. It was something more, too: it put the monarchy, that brilliant edition of everyday life, on television.

To cap it all in 1953, England, with Hutton as its first professional captain, won the Ashes at the Oval. Gordon Richards won his first, and only, Derby on Pinza. But in November the Hungarians taught England a hard soccer lesson, 6–3, at Wembley—the first time a European team had won there. Still, the following year, at Oxford, Bannister became the first man to run the four-minute mile.

It was a time for long-runners. A thriller called *The Mousetrap* opened in November 1952; an agent called James Bond first appeared in Ian Fleming's *Casino Royale* in 1953; Sandy Wilson's *The Boy Friend* and Julian Slade's *Salad Days* both entered the limelight. Suburbia, not socialism, plainly held the key to the future. And it seemed to work.

There were disquieting things. The Mau Mau were active in Kenya, a portent that suburbia's youth might not rely indefinitely on jobs in the colonies. There were still 100,000 troops fighting Chinese guerrillas in Malaya. Britain's Comet, the world's first jet airliner, flew swankily to Johannesburg in May 1952; two years later, Comet wreckage was being fished out of the sea.

Even so, no one blamed Churchill for any of that. The Queen gave him the Garter (which he preferred to a dukedom), the Commons gave him an 80th-birthday portrait by Graham Sutherland and, in April 1955, Churchill resigned, though remaining an MP, in a blaze of glory. The few who grudged him the glory were comforted that a strike denied him the pleasure of reading about it in the papers.

Eden immediately went to the country and won handily over a dispirited Labour party—so dispirited that the Tories even gained a majority of votes in Scotland. But Eden's high reputation was already behind him. Now, an increasingly ill man, he drove himself on to tragedy.

Churchill had turned to summitry because that was what he had done during the war. In turn, Eden was very conscious that his reputation was based on resistance to the dictators of the 1930s. The Middle East was the one remaining part of the world where the Americans, overestimating Britain's strength, left Eden a free hand. He duly warned Bulganin and Khrushchev, when they came to London in April 1956, that Britain would fight to keep its oil there. They seemed impressed.

So it was not inevitable that Eden should come to identify Egypt's Nasser as a 'megalomaniacal dictator' whom he must put down. But when Nasser, rebuffed by the Americans over the financing of the Aswan High Dam, seized the Suez Canal and its receipts in July, Eden actually had no other option.

He was disturbed by the spread of Egyptian influence in the Arab world, to which he attributed the sacking of Glubb Pasha from the Arab Legion in Jordan; he was probably just as rattled by Conservative misgivings after the Tonbridge by-election in June. And so, Eden resolved to strike against Nasser with French and Israeli collusion but, fatally for him, without American approval. Eisenhower was preoccupied with being re-elected and as the Anglo-French expedition reached Suez the Soviets were entering Budapest.

Eden could have survived Labour's intense anti-Suez agitation in the country; he almost certainly had public opinion with him for going in. But the expeditionary force took too long to get there and the Americans put the squeeze on sterling. Eden called a halt with Nasser prostrate but still in power. Whatever support he had for going into Suez, he could not keep it by coming out so soon and having done nothing except confirm Britain's galloping frailty. He resigned the following January.

Suez overflowed everything in Eden's year and nine months, yet there were some intriguing milestones. Calder Hall, the world's first large-scale nuclear power station, began generating. The Silverman bill, abolishing the death penalty, was passed in the Commons. New Zealand House, the first high building in London's West End, started a row. Osborne's *Look Back in Anger* started another. And on 22 September 1955 commercial television, ITV, began. Home life would never be the same again.

Tourist trap.
The London stage thrived,
and it thrived particularly at the Ambassadors
where *The Mousetrap*,
a thriller by Lady Mallowan
(otherwise Agatha Mary Clarissa Christie),
opened on 25 November 1952,
and ran for ever after.
Only a dwindling few no longer knew who did it.

The new Elizabethans.
The young Queen led in
her first classic winner, Carrozza (100–8),
and Epsom took off its hat to her,
and to Lester Piggott, who had assisted.
But the monarchy, like the economy,
lived under constant criticism.
The royals adapted to new times;
much of the economy was noticeably slower.

Now Labour's days seemed numbered. Cripps (above) introduced
a cautious budget after the 1950 election, but he was tired and ill
and had to retire in November. He was replaced by Gaitskell (right),
then 44, who just eight months before had been
a humble minister of fuel and power.
Though Gaitskell had been helping Cripps, his promotion
was something of a surprise and the Bevanite left
sensed in him their most considerable opponent in the fight
for the party's future. Bevan waited four years before declaring,
'I know that the right kind of leader for the Labour party
is a desiccated calculating machine',
but that was what he and his friends thought of Gaitskell all along.
Gaitskell's only budget, in 1951, had to find money
for rearmament for the Korean war. He did not hesitate to charge
for national health teeth and glasses, thereby placing
his hand on the ark of the Bevanite covenant. Bevan, Wilson
and a junior minister, Freeman, resigned. With Bevin and Cripps gone,
Attlee and Morrison failing, Gaitskell was the rising star.
The King had cancer. His family was told, though he and the country
were not. He had an operation to remove a lung in 1951
and seemed better (below) although plainly frail.
He went to his grandson's third birthday party in November,
and recorded his Christmas message for radio
in short takes, to help his voice.

Daily Mirror

THURS OCT. 25 1951

1½ d

FORWARD WITH THE PEOPLE

No. 14,915

Registered at G.P.O. as a Newspaper

WHOSE FINGER?

BIG ISSUES OF 1951

Today YOUR finger is on the trigger

SEE YOU DEFEND

PEACE with SECURITY and PROGRESS with FAIR SHARES

VOTE FOR THE PARTY YOU CAN REALLY TRUST

The 'Daily Mirror' believes that Party is Labour

The general election came on 25 October 1951. That morning the *Daily Mirror*'s front page (left) tried its hardest to stave off Labour's defeat. It was a propaganda masterpiece which had Churchill issuing a writ (though in victory his motto was magnanimity), and it nearly worked. Labour won most votes, the Conservatives most seats. So, a month away from his 77th birthday, the old indestructible man left Chartwell (below) with his wife to return to Downing Street, there to start cabinet-making amid tears and no little confusion. Winston was back.

The King died in his sleep at Sandringham. His valet found him on the morning of 6 February 1952.
The new Queen flew home from Kenya to London airport (left)
to be met by (right to left) Churchill, Attlee, Eden and Woolton.
Three Queens mourned him (above) and a third of a million of his subjects
went past his coffin in Westminster Hall.
His daughter told her first Privy Council,
'My heart is too full for me to say more to you today
than that I shall always work as my father did'.
Sixteen months later, on 2 June 1953, she was crowned at Westminster Abbey.

The new Elizabethan age, as the conceit
of the day went, got off
to a bumpy start. Everyone was delighted,
of course, that Hillary
(right, photographed by Tensing)
had climbed to the top of Everest
just in time for the coronation.
But what was the next British first to be?
It turned out to be the first
British nuclear deterrent. The bomb was
successfully tested in October 1952,
in the Monte Bello islands
off the Australian coast.
The atom bomb had been ordered by Attlee,
without any fuss, so natural
did it seem that Britain should try
to keep up with the greater powers.
Now it was an essential part of Britain's
defence and the British hydrogen bomb
(opposite) was coming along.
From the moment he won the election
Churchill was aware of efforts,
which King George had favoured,
to replace him by Eden.
But Eden had his preoccupations.
Besides being back at the Foreign Office
he was in love with Clarissa Churchill,
the prime minister's niece, and they
were married at Caxton Hall in August 1952.
The reception (below) was naturally at No. 10.
Eden was frequently ill, too.
Each bout gave Churchill the excuse to stay on.
British and Commonwealth troops fought
in Korea with the United Nations (right).
But the war, whose origins appeared simple,
became both more complicated
and more dangerous in British eyes
when the communist Chinese joined in.
Britain, unlike the United States,
had recognized communist China.

It was a relief
when the armistice came in July 1953.
The fogs, the old pea-soupers,
still came down on London (far right) and the big,
smoky cities. In December 1952
fog took 4,000 lives.
The Clean Air Act of 1956
began to change that.
After all, with the passing of the trams
there was no other way for people to get home.

These were early days for liberation. British policy was still set on forming a multi-racial
federation in central Africa, made up of the two Rhodesias and Nyasaland.
This was already unpopular among most blacks, and a conference at Lancaster House in April 1952
was boycotted, except (left, foreground) by a certain Mr J. N. N. Nkomo from Southern Rhodesia.
He was to be independent Zimbabwe's first home affairs minister.
White nerves in Kenya were set on edge by the Mau Mau rebellion among the Kikuyu,
who went in for nasty oath-taking and even nastier killings—of other blacks
much more than whites. Jomo Kenyatta (below left) was seized
and put into detention, though he denied having anything to do with terrorism.
He was to be independent Kenya's first president.
Seretse Khama, chief of the Bamangwato in Bechuanaland, lived quietly
in exile in Surrey with his wife, Ruth, and daughter, Jacqueline.
His offence, in the eyes of the elders both of his tribe and of the Labour government,
had been to marry a white woman. He was to be independent Botswana's first president.

Everything comes to those who wait.
Sweet rationing ended in February 1953,
so Conservatism worked for the kids.
And food rationing went next year
and housewives could throw
their ration books on the fire
at last, after 14 long years.
Gordon Richards (above) won
the coronation Derby on Pinza (5–1).
Although he had been champion jockey
since time knew when, it was his only Derby win.
The new Queen's Aureole was second.
And Stanley Matthews got his cup-winners' medal
at last (below), his virtuosity
and the will of the Wembley crowd
helping Blackpool beat Bolton 4–3.
The public was shocked at,
but delightedly read about, what the police
found in the back garden (above right)
at Rillington Place, Notting Hill.
The trial of John Halliday Christie,
thought to have murdered at least six women,
opened at the Old Bailey in June 1953.

The legal authorities were reluctant
to admit that they had hanged a man,
Timothy Evans, who lived in the house,
for one of Christie's crimes.
Even more shocking was England's defeat, 6–3,
by Hungary at Wembley.
England's defenders could only watch (below)
while the second goal went in.
The pitiable continentals
were teaching them how to play.
The public was shocked, or was told
by the newspapers to be shocked, at Reg Butler's
successful entry, *The Unknown Political Prisoner*
(above right), which won him £4,500.
He need not have minded.
He was to become one of the country's
better, and better-known, sculptors.
And a warrant was issued
for Lord Montagu of Beaulieu, who had sailed
to the United States (right). He came back
to face charges of homosexual practice.
The law, like those on abortion and divorce,
would not be changed for some time.

The powers still disagreed over Germany.
They could not unite it. The Soviet Union
refused to budge from its occupied zone,
which it had turned into a communist satellite.
The West wished to bring its part
of Germany into its defensive system.
In 1954 the Berlin conference (above)
broke down and Dulles, Eden and Bidault
needed to work something out.
Britain, in a rare intervention in Europe,
promised France to station four divisions
and a tactical air force on the continent
to pacify fears of an independent
and rearmed West Germany.
By October the allied occupation was over
and Germany was in Nato.
The bloom was coming off the new age.
The British cinema began to get a name
for industrial disputes (top right) even more
than for box-office successes.
An American star, Ronald Reagan, said the unions
made his one picture in Britain,
The Hasty Heart, enough for him.
And the angry young generation
made itself heard.
John Osborne's *Look Back in Anger*
opened at the Royal Court
in May 1956, with (right)
Kenneth Haigh and Mary Ure.
The bourgeoisie flocked to see.

It was all happening.
Flying saucers
began appearing in earnest.
This one in 1954 (below)
was spotted and drawn
by Stephen Darbishire, aged 13.
He did not meet their leader.
The flying Roger Bannister
was all fact, all right:
the first man
to run the mile
in under four minutes.
Churchill reached his 80th birthday,
still in office,
though now a knight of the garter.
He told the people modestly
that he did not accept
'what many have kindly said',
that he inspired the country
in the war.
'It was the nation and the race
dwelling all round the globe
that had the lion's heart.
I had the luck to be called
on to give the roar.'
But he was not pleased
with Parliament's gift (right),
a portrait by Graham Sutherland.
He felt it made him look decrepit.
Lady Churchill had it burned.
His heir-apparent kept busy.
In February 1955
he was holding hands in Cairo
with the new Egyptian dictator,
Nasser.

Churchill went on 6 April 1955,
having had the Queen to dinner
at No. 10 (left) the night before.
It was the end of more than one age.
He had first 'looked out from my regimental cradle'
and entered politics in Victoria's time.
His going, as it happened, made little stir.
Fleet Street was on strike
so there was quite a demand (below)
for the provincial papers.
Of course, he had nothing to do with television.
When the papers came back (right)
it was to reopen the campaign
to abolish the death penalty.
Ruth Ellis had admitted shooting one of her lovers.
But she was young, good-looking.
She had two children.
Ten years later the Murder Act suspended
the death penalty, as a trial; it did not return.

Daily Mirror

THURS JULY 14 1955

1½d FORWARD WITH THE PEOPLE
No. 18,046

Millions of people are worried about the fate of RUTH ELLIS. Today we ask our readers—

SHOULD HANGING BE STOPPED?

RUTH ELLIS . . . HER EXECUTION HAS SET THE WHOLE WORLD TALKING.

YESTERDAY was not a happy day in Britain. The sun shone but the nation was upset.

At 9 a.m. in Holloway Gaol a woman of twenty-eight suffered death by hanging. Her body was later buried within the precincts of the prison.

Mrs. Ruth Ellis was not a virtuous woman. She admitted shooting one of her two lovers because she thought he was unfaithful. This was the gruesome end to a sordid affair.

Yet few in Britain yesterday felt happy that this mother of two children should lose her life —even though she herself had taken life?

Do the people of Britain believe that the punishment for murder should be CAPITAL PUNISHMENT?

M.P.s would not go past the prison

Are Members of Parliament satisfied that hanging is the expression of the public will?

Some M.P.s were NOT happy yesterday. Some who were to drive past Holloway Gaol on their way to the House of Commons took a different route to avoid the prison.

Five months ago M.P.s debated capital punishment. On a free vote they decided against a suggestion that the death penalty should be suspended FOR AN EXPERIMENTAL PERIOD OF FIVE YEARS and replaced by life imprisonment.

But did this vote mean that the majority of M.P.s were in favour of hanging? They voted against its suspension — not against its abolition.

One man had to decide her fate

How would they have voted on the straight question: Should we abolish the death penalty for good?

How would they vote today?

Because there is a death sentence, one man has a terrible responsibility. In court the witnesses give evidence, the jury return a verdict, the judge passes sentence. They all represent the public conscience. All did their duty at the trial of Ruth Ellis.

But one man—a professional politician who happens to be Home Secretary—had to decide whether this woman should be reprieved.

What an unenviable task.

While this young woman waited in her prison cell one man had to decide whether there should be visited on her the retribution prescribed in a pitiless Biblical phrase:

" And thine eye shall not pity; but life shall go for life, eye for eye, tooth for tooth, hand for hand, foot for foot."

These words from the Old Testament Book of Deuteronomy were written probably 2,500 years ago, before the birth of Christ, by an unknown Jewish scribe.

And the enlightened British nation today still follows the teaching of all those centuries ago.

It is understandable why people in Britain felt uneasy yesterday. In the rush of life the particular case of Ruth Ellis will be forgotten. But the problem of capital punishment remains.

Some murderers attract much public sympathy. There has been more talk about the fate of PRETTY YOUNG Ruth Ellis than there was about the similar fate of UGLY Mrs. Christofi, aged fifty-three, who strangled her daughter-in-law.

But is it unnatural if the execution of a pretty young mother causes public distress?

One fact remains :

Whether a murderess is pretty or ugly.

Whether a murderer is young or old.

Whether a killer attracts public sympathy or not—the lawful penalty is death by hanging.

Time for a change in the Law?

What the Ruth Ellis case has done is to focus attention on the whole problem of capital punishment.

People are asking:

Is hanging degrading to a civilised nation? Has the time come for hanging to be abolished in Britain?

or—

Should hanging be retained as the just penalty for taking life?

The "Mirror" believes that the public should be able to voice its views.

Today we ask readers to give their verdict. There is a voting form in the Back Page.

Please express your opinion on the voting form in the Back Page

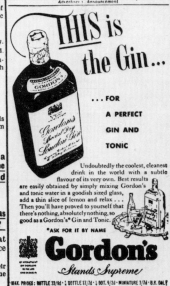

Eden promptly called a general election and duly won it.
It was the first television election and he and his ministers sat,
edgily (above), waiting to be questioned.
They were (appropriately, left to right):
Macleod (health), Butler (chancellor),
Eden, Macmillan (foreign) and Monckton (labour).
The picture the voters saw was as below,
and there were now three times as many television sets as at the last election.
Eden had a majority of 58, the first time in the century
that a government had increased its standing in the country.

In another regular beauty contest
the Miss World hopefuls paraded their smiles
and anything else available (above)
at the Lyceum, London.
It all passed off peacefully.
What the new government, the advertisers and,
it was hoped, much of the public were waiting for
was the arrival of ITV on 22 September 1955.
The potential stars rehearsed,
among them what was called a lady announcer, Shirley Butler.

Group Captain Peter Townsend,
former equerry to George VI,
was touring the world (far right).
On 31 October 1955
Princess Margaret had put out
a statement:
'I would like it to be known
that I have decided not to marry
Group Captain Peter Townsend . . .
Mindful of the Church's teaching
that Christian marriage
is indissoluble, and conscious
of my duty to the Commonwealth,
I have resolved to put these
considerations before any others.'
Townsend had been divorced
on the ground of his wife's
adultery, but that
was not good enough for the churchmen,
or the politicians,
or the leader writers
who interested themselves
in the affair.
Margaret was 25,
had been in love for years,
and did not need
to ask anyone's permission.
But opinion around her
was too strong.
The prime minister
was doing his thing: diplomacy.

Khruschev came to London
to see him (right), and after dinner
with the Labour party
declared himself
a Conservative voter.
What was more important
to mothers (right) was
the start of vaccination
against infantile paralysis,
a crippling scourge
that conventional medicine
could do little about.
There were scares,
but the vaccine worked
and disfigurement
was soon almost forgotten.
Macmillan (centre right)
brought in his one and only
budget. It was notable
for starting Premium Bonds.
Wilson called it 'a squalid raffle',
but later improved the prizes.
England could still teach
the Australians something.
On a wearing pitch
at Old Trafford in July 1956
the spinner, Jim Laker (far right),
took nine wickets for 37
in the first Australian
innings, and all ten for 53
in the second.

But the day before in Egypt,
Nasser, incensed by the withdrawal
of American aid for the Aswan dam,
nationalized the Suez canal.
Eden cabled Eisenhower,
'We are all agreed
that we cannot afford
to allow Nasser
to seize control
of the canal in this way.'

Eden tried to get international backing
to dislodge Nasser
but Eisenhower and Dulles,
with an election coming up, were not helpful.
Eden then sent Selwyn Lloyd (right)
to Paris to agree to an Israeli attack on Egypt,
which would allow Britain and France
to intervene to protect the Suez canal.
The Americans were not told.
Though Gaitskell and Labour protested violently,
with demonstrations
up and down the country (far right),
British troops landed at Port Said (below)
in November 1956 and pushed along the canal.

But American
and United Nations opinion
was strongly opposed;
a run on sterling began;
Eden had to call a halt.
The Soviets, faced
with a nationalist rising in Hungary,
took their chance.
The Red Army went into Budapest
and, though the Hungarians (below)
fought devotedly, in a matter of days
the tanks put communism
firmly back in power.
The UN could not get them out.

Never had it so good

Summoned by the Queen to form a government in January 1957, Harold Macmillan warned her it might not last more than six weeks. But he was much too shrewd to let things slip. He believed he knew, from his years as MP for Stockton in the 1930s, what the working class wanted; and he had equipped himself with a version of Keynesianism (*The Middle Way*) that could give it to them.

He believed, too, that he could get the Americans back. After all, he had an American mother and had worked with Eisenhower at his headquarters in North Africa. Macmillan was wholly professional: he had charm, a good mind and an ear for a good phrase. He was determined to master television, and he did. All this, of course, he hid behind a calculated Edwardian manner.

So Macmillan wooed Ike and, after Ike, Kennedy. He went off to Moscow in his white hat and got Khruschev to agree to a summit in Paris. It was a bitter disappointment that the Soviets then shot down an American U-2 so that Khruschev could break the whole thing up.

In the economy he did not hesitate to put bank rate up to an unheard-of seven per cent to save the pound. Neither did he hesitate to accept the resignations of his Treasury ministers (Thorneycroft, Powell and Birch) when they insisted on keeping public spending down. He dismissed them as 'little local difficulties' and went for economic growth. Cars and other consumer durables boomed. So did the Viscount airliner, selling even in the United States.

When the election came in October 1959, most of the voters forgot Suez and the petrol rationing that had followed it. They agreed that they had 'never had it so good'. Only north-west England, where cotton was fading, and the west of Scotland, where shipbuilding was sinking, turned towards Labour.

It was the apogee of Macmillan's career and his philosophy. He was Supermac. But it all had to be paid for.

The economic success had been built on flimsy foundations. Wage settlements outran productivity. The balance of payments was slipping again. Suburbia did not take to restraint, and the Liberals scored their biggest by-election upset at Orpington in March 1962. But restraint was what the chancellor, Selwyn Lloyd, insisted on in his 'pay pause'.

Lloyd backed it up by the boldest venture yet into Tory economic planning: a National Economic Development Council (Neddy) and a National Incomes Commission (Nicky). Neither got speedy results. Macmillan fretted, then dismissed Lloyd and a third of the cabinet. The sardonic Jeremy Thorpe said, 'Greater love hath no man than this, that he lays down his friends for his life'.

It was a struggle, too, to keep the independent nuclear deterrent credible. Since the Conservatives had given up conscription, the deterrent was declared to be all the more important; it also kept Macmillan at the powers' top table. But the Blue Streak missile had to be abandoned in

Unflappable.
Harold Macmillan had six years,
nine months in No. 10 (and Admiralty House
when No. 10 had to be repaired), the longest
continuous premiership, after Asquith's,
of the century. He brushed aside local difficulty
after local difficulty to general applause
and his own enjoyment
—until he brushed aside Profumo, one too many.

1960; it was too easy for the Soviets to knock out. So the V-bombers would carry on flying equipped with an American missile, Skybolt. When the Americans stopped Skybolt for themselves that seemed to be that. But Macmillan went off to Nassau and got Polaris missiles from Kennedy, to be installed in four nuclear submarines. It pleased the navy.

It did not please de Gaulle who saw it as proof positive that Britain was simply not European. In January 1963 he called off the Brussels negotiations on Britain's bid to join the Common Market. 'England,' he said, 'is insular, maritime ... the nature, the structure, the very situation that are England's differ profoundly from those of continentals.'

This was thoroughly inconvenient for Supermac and his young assistant at the talks, Edward Heath, because they had no alternative plan. And then other troubles came crowding in.

For months there had been rumours that the secretary for war, John Profumo, had gone to bed with a call-girl, Christine

Heads down.
Bingo drew nearly one in five
of semi-skilled and unskilled women
out for a regular flutter
with their friends and neighbours.
It gave them a nice change
when the old man went down the pub,
and it saved a few of the cinemas
that the new commercial television was closing.

Keeler. Keeler also shared her favours with the Soviet naval attaché who, she claimed, had asked her to get military information.

Profumo, with Macmillan sitting beside him, denied this in the Commons. But the stories persisted. The Lord Chancellor was told to inquire. Profumo confessed, 'I have to admit ... that I misled you, and my colleagues, and the House'. Macmillan got a roasting in debate and 27 Tories refused to vote for him at the end of it.

Labour's leader, Gaitskell, died suddenly in January 1963. He had spent years trying to modernize Labour's appeal and had attempted, in vain, to drop Clause IV on nationalization from the party's constitution. Beaten on unilateral nuclear disarmament at the party conference in 1960, he promised to 'fight and fight and fight again to save the party we love'. Next year he won the vote, though the Easter marches from Aldermaston to Trafalgar Square remained compulsory for the left wing.

Now, just when he was coming into his own, he was gone. His successor, Wilson, was politically astute, quick-witted, concealing a conventional mind under left-wing phrases. He made hay with the Tory troubles; all the more when Macmillan resigned in October 1963 to face a prostatectomy. Macmillan was succeeded by Alec Douglas-Home, the 14th Earl of Home, who stepped down from the Lords to take on 'the 14th Mr Wilson', as he neatly put it. There was much more in Douglas-Home than met the eye.

The Crown had not had it particularly good. The Queen had been told she was dowdy by her critics and, in a concession to democracy, she dropped presentation parties for débutantes in 1957. More pertinently, that year she gave her Christmas address on television for the first time.

Change was coming all round. The Wolfenden report said homosexuality was all right between consenting adults. Life peers began in 1958, and so did race riots at Notting Hill. The first stretch of motorway, from Luton to Dunstable, was opened. The Beeching report recommended closing a third of the railways. And *Lady Chatterley's Lover* was pronounced suitable for wives, servants and everyone else to read. Where would it all end?

Macmillan put down his copy
of *Pride and Prejudice*
in No. 11 Downing Street
('very soothing' he said he found it)
and went off to be asked
to form a government.
Like the music-hall
actor-manager inside him,
he had to cheer up
the Conservative party,
and the country.
If Margaret Leighton
and Kay Kendall (right) could do it,
he would stage a revival too,
if necessary right outside
his own front door (far right)
on his return from touring
the Commonwealth in 1958.
He signed up
a strong supporting cast.
There was Nikita Khruschev (below),
who got over a little
diplomatic toothache and agreed,
with Marx and Lenin looking on,
to go to a summit with the West.
There was Dwight D. Eisenhower
who flew over to dine (below right)
and even go on television
with the election coming up.
'Naturally', Macmillan noted,
'I was accused of arranging the visit
for my own electoral purposes.
But although the coincidence
may have been happy,
it was certainly
not by my design.' No, of course not.
Anyway, he won by 100 in October 1959.
Among the new MPs
was Mrs Margaret Thatcher,
then just 33, from Finchley.
But as she arrived, Peter Thorneycroft
(far right) was out of power
and almost out of consideration.
He had walked out on Macmillan
in January 1958 over government spending
and was not forgiven for two years.

Bevan, though a disappointed man,
worked loyally for Gaitskell (above).
He even took on the unilateral disarmers, whom he accused
of wanting to send the British foreign secretary,
'whoever he was, naked into the conference chamber'.
But Gaitskell seemed happier with George Brown (top centre)
as his deputy leader, even though Brown
became much more favourable to Britain
joining the Common Market than he was.
Bevan had kept his admirers on the Labour left,
but by late 1959 he and they knew
that he had cancer, and he died in July 1960.
He had been a great fighter, an impassioned orator
(though not successful on radio or television),
and with him Labour lost part of its heart.

The coming man on the left was Wilson (above).
He had challenged Gaitskell for the leadership in 1960,
the first time the leader had been made to face a vote,
and was badly beaten, 166 to 81.
Gaitskell had held the trade union MPs, but Wilson kept the left.
He did not think he was disgraced.
Wilson was sceptical, too, about the Common Market
in an old-fashioned sort of way.
He wrote, 'We are not entitled to sell our friends and kinsmen
down the river for a problematical and marginal advantage
in selling washing-machines in Düsseldorf.'
Michael Foot was nowhere. He had lost his Plymouth seat in 1955
and vainly canvassed the navy (above left) in 1959.
On Bevan's death he inherited his seat at Ebbw Vale.

The monarchy was having to change.
The Queen saw to that.
In 1957 her Christmas message
was televised from the library
at Sandringham,
where she sat (right)
with family pictures
at her side.
It was the 25th anniversary
of her grandfather's
first radio address.
She had never liked
the presentation of débutantes.
It was boring and antiquated (far right).
The 1958 ones were the last.
She and the Duke
sent their son to school,
something that the royal family
had never done before.

Prince Charles
set off for Cheam,
in Berkshire (right),
with a sticking plaster on his knee.
A royal picture gallery
was opened to the public
at Buckingham Palace in 1962.
Princess Margaret
was instructed
in some finer points
of art appreciation
by the Surveyor
of the Queen's Pictures,
Sir Anthony Blunt (top left).
The royal critics,
Malcolm Muggeridge (far left)
and Lord Altrincham (left),
were not exactly tamed,
but they were loyally shouted down
and were not
really heard from again.

The early American and Russian space flights brought fame
to the giant radio telescope at Jodrell Bank (above)
in the fields near Manchester airport.
Jodrell Bank and its professor, Bernard Lovell,
became household names overnight because they were able to track the shots;
indeed, the radio telescope, ten times more powerful than any other,
was an essential part of the American programme.
Otherwise, Britain's space effort was much on the modest side.
In the rush hour, in fog, a steam train ran into an electric one
at St John's station, near Lewisham in south London, on 4 December 1957.
A flyover bridge collapsed across the wreckage (below), derailing a third train.
Sixty people were killed and over 200 injured.

England set off to defend the Ashes in Australia in the winter of 1958–59
with one of the best fast-bowling attacks ever (above).
Arriving at Perth (left to right): Tyson, Loader, Trueman, Statham and Bailey.
The result: Australia won four out of five.
An Elizabethan aircraft crashed shortly after take-off
at Munich airport on 6 February 1958 (below).
Twenty-two people died, including
seven Manchester United players, returning from a match at Belgrade.
United's manager, Matt Busby, survived—just.
It was the end of the Busby Babes,
the great club side of the 1950s.
But Busby came back to build
the European Cup-winning side of 1967–68.

Trying to make a comeback,
Sir Oswald Mosley,
leader of the Blackshirts
before the war, climbed up
beside the lions
in Trafalgar Square (above)
at a meeting of his Union Movement.
He stood at North Kensington
in the 1959 election
and lost his deposit.
Trying to change, or catch up with,
conventional morals,
Sir John Wolfenden (above right)
and his committee reported
in 1957 that prostitution
was a bad thing on the streets

though permissible indoors,
and homosexuality was all right between
consenting adults, in private of course.
The Mini, designed
by Alec Issigonis (below left),
was the revolutionary car of 1959.
Designed to do 50 miles
to the gallon, the Minis
were by far the most successful idea
of the British mass production industry;
after them, Austin and Morris
all but collapsed.
The transport minister, Ernest Marples,
opened the first 72-mile stretch of the M1,
the London–Birmingham motorway,
in November 1959 (below).

He revelled in all publicity
and was unhappy when
the popular slogan, born of traffic jams,
became Marples Must Go.
Trying to hang on, the cinema
still managed to draw the crowds
for its first nights (above),
but now commercial television,
after an early bad patch,
was getting the fans and the profits.
The queueing went on.
There was a London bus strike (below)
in May 1958, but the government
held out and it collapsed.
The Playboy bunnies lined up, too,
and no one complained about them.

Cattle were slaughtered
across the country in 1960
in the worst outbreak
of foot-and-mouth disease (above)
for many years.
Though there were demands
to go over to the inoculation policy,
as in Europe, slaughter,
which eradicates the disease,
was persisted in.
There was another outbreak in 1967–68.
The lugubrious Tony Hancock,
the epitome
of lower middle-class aspirations,
was at the peak of his reputation
on stage, radio and television (above right).

He pushed himself too hard
and died in Australia in June 1968.
The best-selling British films
were the *Carry On* series,
the brain-child of Gerald Thomas
who kept them going for nearly 20 years.
Sid James did his stuff
with Valerie Van Est (below left)
in *Carry On Doctor*.
Penguin Books had their biggest
success when, at the Old Bailey,
D. H. Lawrence's novel,
Lady Chatterley's Lover,
was adjudged fit to print.
It was a sell-out (top right).
But, despite the belief that freedom

would also end the dirty-book trade,
pornography flourished too.
These were the palmy days
of the *Goons* on radio (below left)
with admirers, and imitators,
from the royal family downwards.
Left to right at the mike:
Milligan, Sellers, Secombe.
Harold Pinter's *The Caretaker*
was a critical success (below)
with Robert Shaw and Donald Pleasance.
It made Pinter's name.
Also making his name, and on the way
to transatlantic fame and fortune,
David Frost (right, with Lance Percival),
the youthful star of BBC's

That Was The Week That Was.
By 1980 he had even persuaded
the powers-that-be to let him
and his friends
run breakfast-time television.

President de Gaulle came to London in April 1960,
on a state visit, rather fuller in the figure
than the old leader of the Free French
who had arrived, without any ceremony, in 1940.
He needed his spectacles, too,
and the Queen waited for him (above)
at the door of Covent Garden before the gala performance.
The visit went well, chiefly because
the Macmillan government had not yet
spoken of trying to join the Common Market; that came a year later.
De Gaulle spoke at the Guildhall and, very movingly,

at Westminster Hall. Macmillan noted,
'On this day at any rate, his affection for Britain
seemed to make him forgetful of his suspicions.'
Princess Margaret and her fiancé,
Antony Armstrong-Jones, went to a charity preview
at the Vaudeville theatre, in the Strand (above).
They were married at Westminster Abbey
in May 1960. There had to be a late substitute as best man,
but otherwise all went well.
Next year, rather reluctantly, he agreed to take the title Earl of Snowdon.
Sixteen years afterwards they separated, and were later divorced.

Each Easter the ban-the-bomb marchers made their way
from Aldermaston, the nuclear research station, to Trafalgar Square.
Most of the young ones walked; some of the big names
attached themselves in time for the publicity.
In 1960 it was claimed
that 100,000 people were in the square.
The Campaign for Nuclear Disarmament had at its peak
the active support of some 50 Labour MPs
and 300,000 enthusiasts in the country.
Among the stalwarts in the front row of the 1962 march were
(left to right): Jacquetta Hawkes,
wife of the novelist, J. B. Priestley; Lord Ritchie-Calder, the scientist;
Canon John Collins; Frank Cousins, general secretary
of the Transport and General Workers' Union;
and Emrys Hughes, the Labour MP for South Ayrshire.
Canon Collins, of St Paul's Cathedral,
was in many ways
the most considerable figure and CND's most effective speaker and debater.
CND began to wane when militants followed Bertrand Russell
and his Committee of 100
in a sit-down in Trafalgar Square in September 1961.
There were over 1,000 arrests. What was more,
the student generation was growing up
to other preoccupations and worries.

97

Archbishops could not
bear to look.
'It Is a Moral Issue',
said *The Times* sternly.
'I begin to suspect
in all these wild accusations . . .
something in the nature
of a plot to destroy
the established system',
the prime minister
wrote to the Queen.
The secretary for war
had got into a scrape
with a model,
or call-girl,
Christine Keeler (below right),
and the story had
everything Fleet Street wanted:
the Russian naval attaché,
shots fired in the night,
a vanished witness,
love letters,
raffish parties,
and still more call-girls,
especially Mandy Rice-Davies
(above right), who also
exposed all she knew
to reporters and,
eventually,
the Lord Chancellor.
Told that another witness
denied her account,
Mandy replied succinctly,
'He would, wouldn't he?'

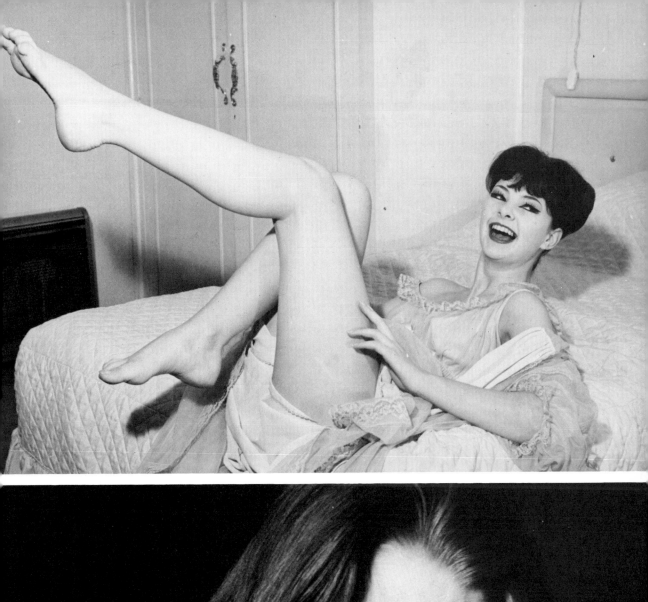

Profumo had been elected to the Commons in 1940, at 25 the youngest MP. He had a brilliant war, left the army a brigadier, and got a junior job in Churchill's government. He moved in society: in the paddock at Sandown races (above) with his wife, the actress Valerie Hobson, and the Queen Mother. In 1960 he became secretary for war under Macmillan. He was told to sell the new regular army and the territorials' emergency reserve now that conscription was over. He made a good, enthusiastic impression (top right). Unluckily for him, however, he made an enemy in the Labour MP, George Wigg, who believed Profumo had tricked him in covering up deficiencies in the army's

operation in Kuwait in July 1961. Wigg resolved to watch Profumo. In 1963 it was he who raised the rumours about Keeler in the Commons. Profumo, having denied the stories about him and then confessed, withdrew altogether from public life. He even lost his membership of the Privy Council (left, in uniform). He devoted himself, much to his credit, to good works in the East End. Dr Stephen Ward, the fashionable osteopath who had first taken Keeler up, took a fatal dose of Nembutal while on trial at the Old Bailey. He was already in a coma (right) when the jury found him guilty of living off Keeler's immoral earnings.

for adventure
and £150 plus

Macmillan had a visit from Kennedy
at Birch Grove in June 1963
which consoled him
after 27 Tories refused to vote for him
at the end of the Commons debate
on the Profumo affair.
Kennedy and he had always got on well (left).
It was their last meeting:
'I can see the helicopter now,
sailing down the valley above
the heavily laden, lush foliage
of oaks and beech at the end of June
. . . Alas, I was never to see my friend again.
Before those leaves had turned and fallen
he was snatched by an assassin's bullet . . .'
Macmillan had still hoped
to fight the next election
but a sudden operation on his prostate
brought his resignation in October.
The Tory chieftains
who heard the news on the platform at Blackpool,
Maudling, Hailsham and Butler (above),
all had their backers.
But Macmillan's blessing,
and a majority of MPs, supported
the Earl of Home (above right)
—Sir Alec Douglas-Home, as he quickly
became to get a seat in the Commons.
It was the Liberals
who felt they were sitting pretty.
Eric Lubbock (right) got a swing
of 26.8 per cent from the Conservatives
at the Orpington by-election in March 1962.
Not even suburbia
was staunch to the Tory cause.

Labour went into the election
in October 1964
very much the favourites after what Wilson
had called '13 years of Conservative misrule'
and the Liberals,
under the dashing Jo Grimond (left),
who had promised
'to march my troops
towards the sound of gunfire',
operated as a diversion
on Sir Alec's flank.
Still, Sir Alec gave them a close fight.
Maudling (below left)
had reflated the economy
although he was becoming apprehensive
about the balance of payments,
and Sir Alec himself
proved a much better campaigner
on the stump (below centre)
than he was on television.
Wilson used every gambit he knew.
He posed with the Beatles (right)
at a Variety Club lunch; after all,
he was a Liverpool MP.
And by the morning of 16 October
he knew (below) he had done it,
by just four seats,
the closest-run thing
for many a long year.

The new head of British Railways, Dr Richard Beeching
(above, at his local station, East Grinstead),
wanted to shut down a third of the track—the third
that brought in only one per cent of the passengers.
Cries of outrage came from every rural halt.
But on 8 August 1963, before the Beeching axe could fall,
the Glasgow–London mail train was ambushed
near Cheddington, Bucks (above right), and it was not until 13 August
that the police found the raiders' headquarters,
a lonely farmhouse, with 60 empty mailbags.
The hunt was on for the missing £2.5 million in used banknotes.
Nowhere (right) was too improbable.
Soon £100,000 was found at Bournemouth,
another £100,000 near Dorking, and £30,000 in a caravan
at Box Hill, Surrey. Someone was talking.
Eventually, the police took in Ronald Arthur Biggs (far right).
It was just the beginning of their acquaintance with him.
He went to every length, escaping to Australia
and then Brazil, and then fathering a Brazilian child,
and even surviving a kidnapping, to avoid
sewing mailbags again.

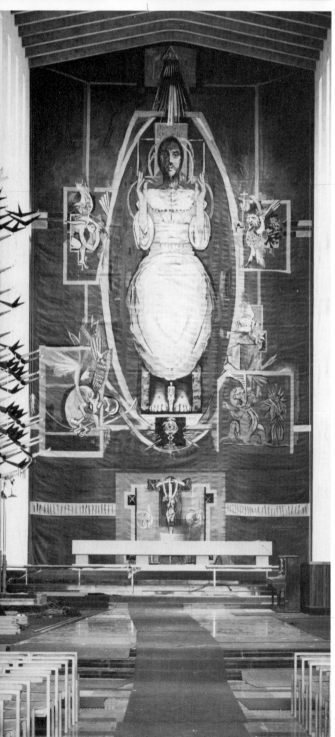

The 1960s were never dull;
though not everything
went as planned.
There was the excitement
of seeing television pictures live from
across the Atlantic
by the satellite Telstar
—except that the very first face (above left)
the British viewers saw on 11 July 1962
was Frederick Kappel's. Fred who?
Why Frederick Kappel, chairman of AT&T,
who built the satellite, that's who.
There was Graham Sutherland's
great tapestry (left)
for the rebuilt Coventry Cathedral;
designer, Basil Spence.
Except that inartistic people
complained that Christ looked pregnant.
Good old Graham Hill looked ecstatic, anyway,
when he won the South African grand prix (above),
and with it the world championship of 1962.
And John Bloom, the housewives' friend,
posed affluently beside
his new Rolls-Royce (above right).
However, it was his Rolls Razor company
that crashed in July 1963,
ending the saga
of the cheap Electromatic washing-machine that
he imported from Holland at £29
and sold in Britain for £44.

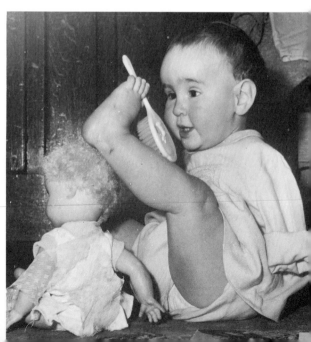

That sort of luck couldn't last.
Rolls had a deficiency of £4 million.
The James Bond films made millions
for the American producers Harry Saltzman
and Cubby Broccoli, especially
when Bond was played
by Sean Connery (top right),
with Luciana Paluzzi in *Thunderball* (1965),
directed by Terence Young.
Mary Quant (flying away
at London airport, right)
hit the jackpot with her fashion design.
Suddenly, nearly everybody
was wearing Quant-style clothes.
The others just went to Carnaby Street.
Rudolf Nureyev came in
from the Soviet Union to dance
at Covent Garden with Margot Fonteyn (below),
with Sir Frederick Ashton directing.
And, unhappily, the thalidomide drug
that promised help to pregnant mothers
turned out to have disastrous effects
on their children.
Although many, like young
Richard Satherley (below left)
showed great dexterity, it was obvious
that generous compensation was in order;
after public pressure,
led by the *Sunday Times*,
the sellers, Distillers, paid up.

The rockers, implacable foes of the mods
whom they habitually fought
every Easter weekend and other times,
favoured leather gear
and lived much in the saddle of big,
noisy and increasingly anachronistic
British motor-bikes.
They even congregated to be blessed
by a ton-up vicar at St Martin-in-the-Fields,
Trafalgar Square (left),
when they promised to help a campaign
for the starving overseas.
Henry Cooper, Britain's best heavyweight,
laid one on Mohammed Ali
in June 1963 (above left),
though Ali then got up to win.
Yorkshire's Freddie Trueman
became the first to take
300 wickets in Test cricket.
He did it (above) against the Australians
at the Oval in August 1964.
Asked if the record would be broken
he said, 'If anyone does
he'll be bloody tired.'
Britain's Audrey Hepburn starred
in the Hollywood version of the hit musical,
My Fair Lady (right, with
the designer, Cecil Beaton).
But culture of another sort
had to be stopped at the docks.
Pornographic paperbacks
were being brought into swinging London
(above right) labelled
Educational Books or even Bibles.

The white heat of Wilson

Harold Wilson seemed to personify what the British were looking for. He was young, only 48—much the youngest prime minister of the century. He was clever and classless and adept on television. He seemed to speak the language of applied science, of the white-coated technicians masterminding 'the white heat', as he put it, of 'the scientific revolution' in Britain. Certainly Wilson, what he did and what he left undone, dominated two decades of our lives.

He wanted to be trusted: after all, he smoked a pipe in public. But he never was quite trusted. He only just squeaked home in his first general election in 1964. His majority was four; eventually it was eroded to one. He won again, decisively, in 1966. But he lost four years later and his last two victories in 1974 were inconclusive, or nearly so.

This may actually have suited his style. It was easier to keep Labour together when every vote counted. He enjoyed sudden crises, stratagems, eleventh-hour solutions. For him, a week really was a long time in politics. But in his heart he must have enjoyed the 1966 triumph best; that year, England won the World Cup, too.

It was Wilson's optimism that kept him going. Faced with Ian Smith's UDI in Rhodesia, he thought sanctions could do the trick in weeks rather than months. Then he thought he could get Smith to compromise in their sea-going talks on board *Tiger* and *Fearless*. Then he thought the oil companies really would respect the money the navy was spending to block the Beira pipeline.

He hoped to bring Lyndon Johnson and the Soviets together over Vietnam; he even sent his personal envoy, Harold Davies (then joint parliamentary secretary to the Ministry of Pensions), all the way to Hanoi to knock their heads together in 1965. It all made headlines. It all came to nothing. And in November 1967 de Gaulle made very sure that Wilson's attempt to get into Europe also came to nothing.

Wilson came to power promising 'one hundred days of dynamic action'. For the foundering economy left by the Tories

Diplomacy at sea.
Wilson (left) and Smith (second from right) at the Sunday service on board HMS *Fearless*, at Gibraltar in October 1968, the second of their inconclusive naval meetings to try to settle Rhodesia. They talked pleasantly enough for 30 hours, chiefly about franchises, but they were still divided.

(with an £800 million deficit in the balance of payments) there was an immediate surcharge of 15 per cent on imports, a 'declaration of intent' (later a policy) on prices and incomes, and a national plan to increase production by 25 per cent in five years.

But nothing went right. The lengthy dock strike in 1966 'led by a tightly-knit group of politically-motivated men' (by which he meant communists) resulted in everything being 'blown off course'. Severe deflation was the only way to stop devaluation—until 1967 when there was devaluation from $2.80 to $2.40.

Wilson went on television to reassure the nervous, blandly denying that 'the pound . . . in your pocket or purse or in your bank has been devalued'. He sacked his chancellor, Callaghan, and brought in Jenkins who put up taxes and cut public spending in two years' hard slog so that exports would rise and imports fall.

In time, this succeeded. But Wilson, Jenkins and the employment secretary, Barbara Castle, wished to go further: they wanted to reduce the unions' ability to strike for higher wages. They called their policy *In Place of Strife* but strife was precisely what it caused between the Labour movement and the government. Callaghan was with the movement. The government backed down.

There were other headaches. As black immigration spread, Enoch Powell raised the voice of white recalcitrance, 'Like the Roman, I seem to see the River Tiber foaming with much blood'. Powell was immediately condemned and dropped from the Conservative shadow cabinet. But he got 100,000 letters in support and he did not let himself be forgotten.

Then, in 1969, Northern Ireland exploded. A civil rights march across the province was broken up by police who suspected it of being a front for Catholic unity with the south. The radical Bernadette Devlin won the Mid-Ulster by-election; there were riots in the Catholic Bogside district of Londonderry; the police were driven out and British troops went in. The worst had happened.

There were new faces in politics. Douglas-Home stepped down with dignity and, in the Conservatives' first leadership election, Heath came top. He was the prototypal new Tory: a grammar-school prize-boy, reforming, abrasive. Those who voted for him hoped he would out-Wilson Wilson. He did not.

Grimond had enough of leading the Liberals and Thorpe took over. Young David Steel arrived after a by-election; and so, ominously for Labour, did Winnie Ewing, the first Scottish Nationalist for 22 years, and Gwynfor Evans, the first-ever Plaid Cymru man.

In October 1966, the collapse of a pit heap at Aberfan in south Wales, engulfing a school and the children in it, reminded the rest of the country of the continuing hardships in the valleys. There the mines were closing; a quarter of the houses were pre-1891; and half the homes in the Rhondda still had outside lavatories.

These were the Plaid's best years in the valleys, with big by-election swings; a militant fringe went further with mock guerrilla training and occasional bombs. Bombs went off just before Prince Charles was invested as Prince of Wales at Caernarvon on a damp day in July 1969; but most of Wales loved the ceremony and the town took in a million tourist dollars.

These were seafaring years. Francis Chichester sailed single-handed round the world and the new Conservative leader went off to win the Sydney-Hobart race. So it was slightly tactless of the ailing Cunard company to sell off its aged *Queens, Mary* and *Elizabeth*, in 1967 and even worse that the new *QE2* had an eccentric maiden voyage. Concorde, the supersonic airliner, flew for the first time and the hovercraft started service between Dover and Boulogne.

Also starting: British heart transplants, legal abortions, breathalyser tests for drivers, and votes at 18. Decimal currency was announced. *The Times* put news on its front page and was bought by the Canadian, Roy Thomson; the left-wing *Sun* was bought by the Australian Rupert Murdoch, and put nudes on its third page. It was the *Sun* that flourished.

There died, shortly after 8 am on 24 January 1965, Winston Leonard Spencer Churchill, KG, OM, in his 91st year. He had been prime minister for eight years and eight months; an MP for 62 years. Macmillan got the right words, 'The greatest heart in England had ceased to beat'.

Barbara's breathalyser. Barbara Castle,
a non-driving transport minister,
was determined to reduce
the deaths caused by sheer drunkenness.
The breathalyser, plus her flair
for publicity and a £300,000 advertising
campaign in October 1967, caused dismay
at closing-time but it began to do something.

Wilson, once in No. 10, was soon off
and running in the international
diplomacy business.
He flew to New York
to address the United Nations
in December 1965,
and then south to Washington
to see Lyndon Johnson (right).
For Wilson it was a chance to talk
about Rhodesia, for LBJ about Vietnam.
Wilson had had cause to be busy.
His first choice as foreign secretary,
Patrick Gordon-Walker (below left,
at his Foreign Office desk),
was beaten at his Smethwick constituency
in the 1964 election,
chiefly because of the immigration issue.
(Wilson called the Tory victor
a 'parliamentary leper'.)
A vacancy was made
in the safe Labour seat at Leyton
but Gordon-Walker,
a forlorn campaigner,
lost again in January 1965.
He was soon out of that chair.
What Wilson found hard
was dealing with Rhodesia's Ian Smith.
Smith came to London in October 1965
to see Wilson and his colonial secretary,
Arthur Bottomley (right),
but they got nowhere.
Britain insisted,
as it had done all along,
on five points.
These were that there must be
unimpeded progress towards majority rule,
that there must be guarantees
against any falling away,
that there must be
an immediate improvement
in the blacks' political status,
that there must be progress
towards ending racial discrimination,
and that independence on these terms
must be acceptable
to the blacks as well as the whites.
Wilson flew to Salisbury himself
at the end of the month
but failed there, too.
On 11 November Smith declared
Rhodesia independent.
The British answer was trade sanctions,
which Wilson hoped would end
the rebellion within
'weeks rather than months'.
He was wrong.
But he was right
about the British electorate.
They put him back in No. 10
with a majority of 96
when he called
the election in March 1966.

A mountain of black slag
moved above the mining village
of Aberfan,
just south of Merthyr Tydfil,
on 21 October 1966
and engulfed the school
and houses nearby.
There were 144 dead,
116 of them children.
The rescuers worked through the night
and when dawn came
they were left with the wreckage of their,
and their children's, lives (top left).
A week later 82 of the children
were buried together in one,
long mass grave
along the hillside (below left).
The cause was found to be water
seeping into the coal tip.
The chairman of the coal board,
Lord Robens, said at the end of the inquiry
that he accepted full responsibility.
The tribunal's chairman
told him if he had done that
at the outset it would have saved
months of evidence-taking.
A Liberian tanker, the *Torrey Canyon*,
ran aground on the Sevenstones Reef,
near the Scilly Isles (top right),
in broad daylight and in perfect weather
on 18 March 1967.
She carried 117,000 tons of crude oil.
When she broke her back
thousands of tons of oil came away,
spreading eastwards to the coasts of Cornwall
and along the English Channel.
Wilson gave the order to bomb the wreck.
The first two sticks of bombs,
in broad daylight and in perfect weather, missed.
But the third hit its target
and the oil caught fire.
Still, it needed even more bombs
the next day to finish the job off.
The prime minister thought the navy had done a great job.
Donald Campbell, son of Sir Malcolm,
the pre-war record-breaker,
tried to improve his world water-speed record
on Coniston Water in 1967.
His *Bluebird* touched over 300 mph,
then leapt into the air,
somersaulted backwards and sank (right).
Campbell was killed.

A sea-faring people had much to add
to the sagas of the rough island race.
Or something like that anyway.
There was Sir Francis Chichester in *Gypsy Moth IV*.
Flying the white ensign (above), he returned to Plymouth
after sailing single-handed round the world.
Soon even women were doing it.
The last of the great Cunarders, the *QE2*,
was launched by the Queen
at the old John Brown shipyard at Clydebank (top right).
Unfortunately, her engines had a well-publicized
bad time during trials, and Brown's itself
disappeared into the loss-making Upper Clyde Shipbuilders.
A reputation had been destroyed.

Still, there was the new hovercraft,
the first cross-Channel service
between Ramsgate and Calais (above right),
which began in the summer of 1966.
And, of course, the stirring victory
over the rebels on the Caribbean island of Anguilla,
who had dared to throw out
a British under-secretary
in March 1969, did much for morale.
Troops and metropolitan police were despatched
and met no resistance on the beaches (right),
except from the cameramen
who had got there beforehand.
The bobbies loved it.

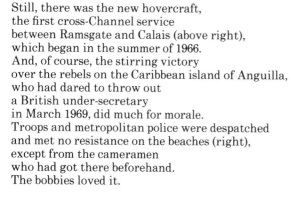

Wilson had always set his face
firmly against devaluing the £1,
although the idea of helping exports
in this way had been urged on him
by his advisers and by George Brown
and the Department of Economic Affairs.
He had refused to listen. Now, on
18 November 1967, he had to eat
his words. The £1 was devalued
to $2.40, a fall of 14 per cent,
and bank rate went up to eight per cent.
The City messengers
were fleet of foot with bad news (above)
and the voters read it,
glumly, in their Sunday papers (above right).
Wilson felt that he must defend
and explain himself.

He went on television
on Sunday evening (left) conscious,
as he said, that 'there would be timid
and frightened people thronging
the post office and bank counters'.
To them he said that the pound
in the pocket would not be
devalued. He even said that
food prices would go up.
But he lived to regret it all.
The only politician
to get greetings telegrams that month
was Winnie Ewing, the Scottish Nationalist,
who unseated Labour
in the Hamilton by-election (right).
Not for the first or the last time,
the Nationalists felt they were on their way.

Beatlemania
was certainly catching.
The young fans had to be held
back at the gates
of Buckingham Palace (far right)
when the famous four
went to collect their MBEs
from the Queen in October 1965.
The award, a Wilson idea,
had been justified
for services to exports,
which the Beatles certainly gave,
but several
less well-known holders
returned theirs in protest.
Perhaps the Beatles
were just too successful.
The Beatles' first two films,
A Hard Day's Night and *Help!*,
were enormously popular.
They were made
in just over a year
by Richard Lester,
and made his reputation
as well as confirming theirs.
At last, a road bridge
was thrown across
the River Severn (right)
as were others
across other estuaries.
There was politics in this,
naturally.
The Conservatives took credit
for the Forth road bridge;
Labour was helped
to win the Hull North by-election,
the prelude
to the 1966 general election,
by a promise to build
the Humber bridge.
But no one promised
to keep steam going.
Paddington's last steam engine,
the *Clun Castle*,
pulled out on its final journey
to Bristol (right)
on 27 November 1965.

The Concorde was going to be Britain's,
and France's, world-beater.
When Labour had thought
of killing the project
back in 1964,
it found the French insisting on damages.
Still, the cost of building Concorde
went on and on and up and up.
The Queen went to BAC at Bristol
to see it (below),
but there were growing doubts
about whether anyone really
meant to buy it.

In July 1966 England
nearly threw it away at Wembley.
The Germans
equalized in the last 30 seconds
of the World Cup final,
to the horror of
(in the darker jerseys, left to right)
Cohen, Moore, Wilson,
Banks and Jackie Charlton
and most of the country
watching on television.
Still, in extra-time
England did it, 4–2,
and London (right)
was well pleased and over the moon.

The mini-skirt still persisted around town and even seemed to get briefer (left).
But toplessness, though briefly tried, was put down by the law.
The weather probably wasn't good enough.
The prime minister showed a leg every summer (above) in his Scilly Isles empire.
He even held press conferences that way.
But women's liberation was on the march. Prisoners' wives,
including those of two of the great train robbers,
were told to leave the authorities their photographs so that their identity
could be checked on visiting days. This blatant sexism
was too much:
they protested (above right) about being the governor's sex objects.
Nuns were in evidence at many anti-abortion rallies.
Those at Birmingham (centre right) looked as
if they enjoyed their unaccustomed day out.
The Miss World contest naturally drew the reformers' ire.
Still, they were not exactly as non-conformist as their placards said.
Even on a chilly night outside the Albert Hall
most of the Women's Liberation Workshop (right)
stayed loyal to their mini-skirts.

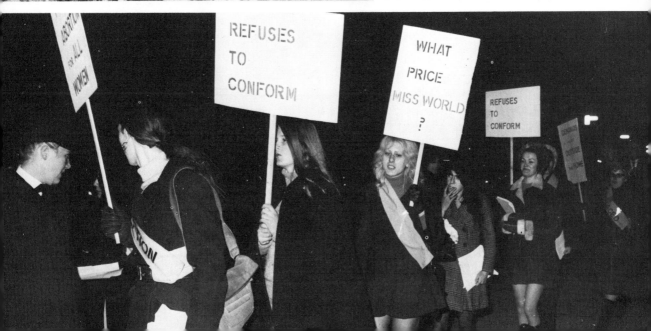

The anti-Vietnam war protestors
marched peacefully to Hyde Park
on 27 October 1968,
but a breakaway group made a dead set
at the United States embassy in Grosvenor Square.
After a struggle
they were repulsed by the police.

It was a time for backing Britain.
Patriots put their convictions (left)
where they showed.
Unfortunately,
it didn't seem to do too much
for the balance of payments.
Britain's heart-transplant team (below)
flew the flag too.
They beamed all over their faces
(left to right, Donald Longmore,
Donald Ross and Keith Ross)
when they announced on 4 May 1968
that the first British transplant
was successful.
And Concorde,
which the British taxpayer
was backing to the hilt
and beyond, was triumphantly rolled out
of its hangar for the first time
in September 1968 (below right).
It was thought to be a good augury
that Pan-Am had not only
taken out an option to buy,
it had even printed
match covers (right) saying so.
Five years later Pan-Am
was the first airline to cancel.

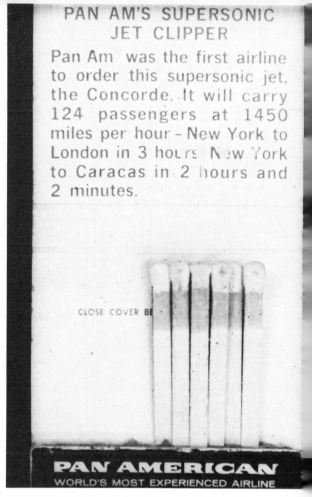

PAN AM'S SUPERSONIC JET CLIPPER

Pan Am was the first airline to order this supersonic jet, the Concorde. It will carry 124 passengers at 1450 miles per hour – New York to London in 3 hours. New York to Caracas in 2 hours and 2 minutes.

CLOSE COVER BE

PAN AMERICAN
WORLD'S MOST EXPERIENCED AIRLINE

Wilson impressed on the liberal Unionist prime minister,
Captain Terence O'Neill, on
4 November 1968,
that urgent reforms were needed in Northern Ireland:
in the local government franchise, in housing allocations,
and in appointing an ombudsman to hear complaints
against the Stormont government.
O'Neill promised to try (top left)
but though his will was undiminished, his authority was running out.
Catholic civil rights demonstrations and rioting had begun.
By August 1969, the Royal Ulster Constabulary
had lost control in the Bogside, Londonderry,
and were exhausted. Protestants took their revenge on Catholics
in west Belfast, street barricades went up and buses were hijacked and burned.
There was nothing for it but to put the troops in (above left).
For the moment the Catholics welcomed them.
The catalyst in the Catholic community was Bernadette Devlin (above),
a civil-rights militant from Queen's University, Belfast,
who won the Mid-Ulster by-election in April 1969.
She jumped to prominence not only in the Commons
but in organizing resistance to the police
in what came to be called Free Derry (right).
The bitterness of generations had welled over again.

VOTE McCANN
YOU ARE NOW ENTERING FREE
DERRY
HUME
T.H.
DERRY
OCT

Peter Hain was an insistent campaigner
to stop the next South African tour
of Britain (above) in 1970.
Under government pressure
and the threat of disturbances
the Cricket Council decided
'with deep regret . . .
they had no alternative but to accede'
The Springboks' rugby tour
had gone ahead in 1969,
although the demonstrators
made their feelings known
at Twickenham (below);
still, rugby loyalists
managed to debag a few of them.

Basil d'Oliviera,
the South African-born all-rounder
who came to England in 1962
to play for Worcestershire (above),
made too many runs
—especially 158 against Australia—
for him not to be offered
a place on MCC's
South African tour in 1968:
whereupon the South African authorities
said a Cape Coloured player
would not be welcome
—and the tour was abandoned.

Other race relations
were not quite so strenuous.
The police wanted to recruit
from the black community,
and PC Norwell Roberts
was the first to join
the metropolitan force.
He met a client (above)
at Covent Garden market.

The immigrant community
settled down (above),
a majority in parts of Birmingham,
Bradford and other cities,
and in its own districts of London.
The older people were orderly,
but sensitive to Powell's speeches
and to changes
in the immigration laws;
its youth in Brixton and Bristol
clashed with police
whom it thought
unnecessarily unsympathetic.

It began to look a different country.
Dutch elm disease struck at the trees,
moving steadily northwards across the land.
The dead stood accusingly (above) by the roadside;
householders had to pay to have theirs cut down and removed.
The vogue for high-rise council flats had never been exactly popular,
except with planners trying to save land and costs.
Parents with young children and old people who found the lifts not working
were told it was an efficient way of dealing with the housing shortage.
That was until the collapse of part of the 22-storey
prefabricated block at Ronan Point, in Canning Town (above right).
More than 200 other blocks had to be looked at in a hurry.
Centre Point, the 33-storey office block at St Giles Circus, London (above far right),
stayed resolutely empty. No one could afford the rent—
until the CBI eventually did. But the property value kept on rising.
Spaghetti Junction, officially the Gravelly Hill interchange,
just outside Birmingham (right), marked the spot
where motorways met and wiped the floor with everything else.
It cost £8 million.

138

In the end, Wilson stumbled into
the general election of June 1970.
He called it (left, at his first
election press conference)
because the local elections
had gone surprisingly well for him
and Labour was, for the first time in years,
ahead in the opinion polls.
In fact, as the campaign went on,
Wilson went so far ahead in the polls
that it almost seemed
he had stopped campaigning.
This was quite a turnaround.
It owed much to the tough budgets
of his chancellor, Roy Jenkins
(below left, on the front bench),
which began to produce
unaccustomedly good balance
of payments figures.
Wilson's particular success
was to keep a very able and volatile
cabinet more or less together.
It cost him some sleep.
The combative Barbara Castle (right)
took on the unions in *In Place of Strife*,
and lost. She had badgered
and pestered Wilson
but he took it philosophically
and would never hear a word against her.
Denis Healey (below,
with RAF luminaries Portal, Harris and,
standing, Barnes Wallis)
was sent to the Department of Defence,
where he was a strong
secretary of state for nearly six years.
Despite Healey's hankering
for the Foreign Office,
he was not moved.
And Wilson took into his cabinet,
as minister of technology,
the ambitious and bright Tony Benn
(below right, boarding
his executive jet for Moscow),
'I suggested to him
he should go easy on publicity'.

Enoch Powell had been the first to speak out openly
against black immigration and had effectively ended
his own chance of getting to the top of the greasy pole.
He had said, 'In 15 or 20 years the black man
will have the whip hand over the white man',
and that seemed likely to be true in parts of the big cities.
He had said, 'We must be mad' to allow immigration to go on.
He had spoken of the Tiber 'foaming with much blood'.
Heath sacked him from the shadow cabinet
but Powell kept a strong following in the country,
especially among the depressed working class which felt its jobs
and its homes most at risk. Now, in the general election (below),
he campaigned vigorously for the Conservatives
with particular impact in his own heartland, the West Midlands.
When the votes were counted there was a swing to the Conservatives
of ten per cent, over twice the national average,
in six seats in and around the Black Country towns
of Dudley and Wolverhampton. Powell felt he had done as much as anyone
to get Heath elected. He waited for results.

Society bowed to the new.
The Rolling Stones were the rage
for those who found the Beatles insipid.
The five, in pseudo-Elizabethan outfits (above),
gave a beggars' banquet (left to right:
Brian Jones, Keith Richard, Mick Jagger,
Bill Wyman and Charlie Watts),
but beggars they certainly were not.
The Church of England moved with the times.
The former England batsman,
the Reverend David Sheppard, became
the Bishop of Woolwich (above right,
with the Archbishop of Canterbury,
Dr Michael Ramsey) in October 1969,
just six years after
his last Test innings.
The previous bishop, Dr John Robinson,
had made the headlines too.
His book, *Honest to God* (1963),
questioning the traditional ideas
of the deity, sold a million.
There were robes and uniforms
at Caernarvon when Prince Charles

was invested by his mother
as Prince of Wales in July 1969 (right),
but for most it was
a lounge-suit-and-best-hat sort of a day.
The centre of attention
wore his uniform as Colonel-in-Chief
of the Royal Regiment of Wales.
He was not asked to wear 'the preposterous rig'
of his immediate predecessor,
the Duke of Windsor, in 1911.
The Duke of Norfolk, in charge of the ceremonial,
was kept on a tight budget.
The hippies arrived. Some were contemplative.
Sir Mark Palmer (far right, below),
a fifth baronet and former Queen's pageboy,
led a group
seeking peace in the West Country.
Others less so. The hippy girl
arriving at Waterloo station
(above right) in August 1970,
was on her way to the Isle of Wight,
seeking a full-blasting,
mind-blowing pop concert.

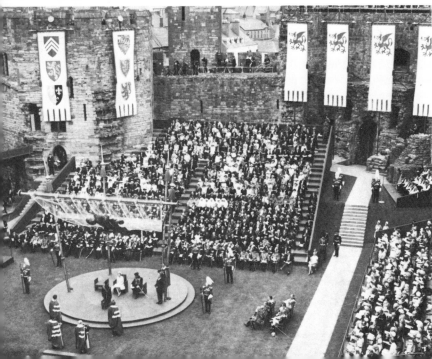

Waiting for nurse

Ted Heath's victory in June 1970 was a surprise to almost everyone but himself. This made him the master of his cabinet. It also seemed to make him indifferent to public opinion: unaware of the need to persuade people to accept the policies on Europe, local government, industry and the unions that he was sure they had elected him to carry out.

He had the people's respect, not their affection. When he got caught in the fight with the miners in the winter of 1973–74, they worked the three-day week and kept production higher than it was to be for years. But he had lost them. He had tried too much, too soon.

Heath got Britain into Europe at last, squaring both Pompidou and most of his own party. In October 1971 the free vote in the Commons saw a Labour split with Jenkins leading 69 Labour MPs into the government lobby. But the business was far from over. Wilson pledged that a Labour government would hold a referendum; both that and the alienation of Powell, who told Tory anti-marketeers to vote Labour, added to Heath's two election defeats in 1974.

When the referendum came in 1975 it was nearly a walkover: 67.2 per cent voted Yes. Heath campaigned gamely, but it was probably Wilson who swung the decisive Labour votes.

It was Heath who, grasping the nettle after Bloody Sunday in Northern Ireland, abolished Stormont and Unionist rule. This did not stop the IRA, which concluded it was winning. But in 1973 Heath and Whitelaw did get moderates—both Unionist, like Faulkner, and Catholic, like Fitt and Hume—to serve together in a power-sharing executive in Belfast. A Unionist general strike, mishandled by Wilson, toppled the executive in May 1974. There was nothing for it but a return to direct rule ... and bombs and bullets on both sides of the Irish Sea.

The first blow to Heath's economic policies was the sudden death of the chancellor, Macleod, a month after the election. With-out him, the government lost its voice. It came in opposed to controls on pay and prices and opposed to subsidies for 'lame duck' industries. The threat of a million unemployed turned Heath right round.

He ended up by nationalizing the bankrupt Rolls-Royce and running a tight, yet largely successful, incomes policy which it took the miners to break. He had meant to reform trade-union law. He ended up with increased strikes and unrest and the most violent picketing since the 1920s. It was the last irony that, before North Sea oil could be brought ashore, he had to face the doubling of the world oil price.

Wilson, back again but powerless, tore up the new union law and let wage inflation rip. By June 1975, weekly wage rates were rising by 33 per cent, prices by 26 per cent and industrial production was down 9 per cent on a year before. Eventually, the union leaders, Jones and Scanlon, agreed to a £6-limit on rises. The so-called 'social contract' on which Wilson had been elected was no longer heard of. Unemployment rose to 1.5 million; the £1 fell to $1.56½.

It was widely said that the day of the two main parties was over, and the Liberals (who had got more than 6 million votes in February 1974) hoped for great things. When, under Callaghan, Labour's exiguous majority disappeared, Steel agreed to a Lib-Lab pact in March 1977.

This put off the general election and gave time for the economy to do better. It also let Labour turn back the Nationalists in Scotland and Wales. But more pay restraint did not please the unions and Callaghan had to go into the election of May 1979 with a winter of flying pickets and various Fleet Street horror stories in everyone's mind. He campaigned bluffly but had no chance.

Margaret Thatcher was the only Tory of consequence who dared stand against Heath for the leadership. When she had seen the men off, she was claimed by the party's right wing as one of their own. She believed in self-help; after all, she was a grocer's daughter. She was committed to the view that control of the money supply, not control of wages, was the way to reduce inflation. She was firm against communism which brought her what she took as a tribute from Moscow, 'the iron lady'. She made the right noises on immigration, law and order.

But this was not the whole story. Though she could speak dismissively of 'the wets' in her cabinet, she was careful not to break with them over unions or immigration; abroad, she successfully submerged her instincts, at her foreign secretary's prompting, on both Europe and Rhodesia. She appeared to see herself as Britain's stern nurse, trying devotedly to get the patient up after much too long a stay in bed.

The emergence of a leader identified with the Tories' ideological right further encouraged the ideological left in the Labour party to make Labour MPs more answerable to their radical management committees in the constituencies and to end the MPs' monopoly in choosing the party leader. This, in turn, brought the leadership to the old Bevanite and Tribunite rebel, Michael Foot. It also, in 1981, prompted the launching of a new, moderate Labour grouping under Roy Jenkins and Shirley Williams. Whether or not all this helped the ambitions of that incorruptible of the left, Tony Benn, remained to be seen.

There was not a happy ending for Jeremy Thorpe, hounded from the Liberal leadership and into court by an accuser who claimed a past homosexual relationship; though Thorpe was cleared of conspiracy to murder, he was out of politics. Nor was there a happy ending for that once-bright Conservative star, Reggie Maudling, who resigned as Home Secretary in 1972 on the collapse of the Poulson company; he died with his name cleared but would have had no future. A former Labour minister, John Stonehouse, disappeared but was brought back in disgrace. Lord Lucan, said to have murdered the nanny, was not found.

And who did well? Certainly Welsh rugby, winning four successive triple crowns; Red Rum winning three Grand Nationals; Coe, Ovett and Wells winning Olympic gold medals on the track; and Virginia Wade who, at last, won Wimbledon.

The protesters. It was more than Women's Lib.
Women civil servants of the genteeler sort took their place
on Whitehall's militant picket lines
for the first time against Margaret Thatcher in March 1981.
From the East End, Rose Davis proclaimed
her husband's blamelessness in August 1975,
and her helpers dug up the pitch at Headingley,
abruptly ending the third Test against the Australians.

The vanishing country.
Urban Britain turned a West Riding vet, James Herriot (out with his dogs),
into a runaway best-seller and the BBC put his stories
of the old days in the Yorkshire dales into the top of the ratings.
It seemed a last cry against the mechanized,
uniform, factory-farm land that had taken over.

When the first result,
from Guildford,
came in on election night,
18 June 1970,
it was a shock: the swing
was to the Conservatives,
and a big enough one (5.5 per cent)
to give Labour the old heave-ho.
Wilson, at his hotel suite
in Liverpool, closed the door
on reporters.
When the full results were known
the Conservatives had made

66 net gains, the biggest
turnaround since 1945.
Wilson made his way
back to London by car
through the night.
Most of the country watched
the upset on television,
although thousands (above)
went down to Trafalgar Square
to watch television there.
It is hard to break the British
of a habit like that.
One habit was broken

in 1970, though.
For the first time
18-year-olds had the vote,
and at least one (above right)
made sure she was there
when the polls opened at 7 a.m.
The local MP in Bexley was ecstatic (right).
For Ted Heath it was victory
after five hard years,
often disastrous opinion polls,
and the open belief
of his friends that he could not do it.
Now he had.

The new prime minister
was a bachelor,
the first since Balfour,
and determined
to stay that way.
There was nothing much
the press photographers
could do except snap him
with women
whenever and wherever
they could. He didn't mind.
So there was the young lady
who helped on board
Morning Cloud (far left).
There was the mayor's daughter
who danced the Gay Gordons (left)
at the party conference.
And, scoop of scoops,
there were all the Tory lady MPs,
actually posing (below left)
beside the leader himself.

He, of course,
kept up his conducting duties
at Broadstairs Christmas carols.
He liked that better.
The most formidable
of the Tory women
was the education secretary,
Margaret Thatcher.
She had all the right experience
for dealing with
a young delegation (above)
wanting more nursery schools.
But the government's first budget,
in October 1970,
cut 6d (2½p) off income tax,
partly at the expense of
ending free school milk.
Mrs Thatcher was promptly called
'the milk snatcher' by Labour,
and six London boroughs
supplied the milk
on the rates.

SAY "NO" TO COMMON MARKET

ANTI-COMMON MARKET LEAGUE
YOUR COUNTRY NEEDS YOUR HELP NOW
SIGN THE NATIONAL COMMON MARKET PETITION

SAY "NO" TO COMMON MARKET

DO YOU WANT TO BE GOVERNED FROM BRUSSELS? IF NO
Sign The National PETITION to the QUEEN
Anti Common Market League

Heath pressed the bid to join the Common Market.
He saw Pompidou, de Gaulle's successor,
at the Elysée (top left) in March 1971
and got his blessing.
There was strong opposition in the Commons
and the country from left and right.
Michael Foot (above) shared his anti-market platform
with a Tory of Tories, Sir Derek Walker-Smith (far right).
But Labour was the more badly split,
and 69 Labour marketeers
voted with the government in October.
In Brussels on 22 January 1972
Heath signed Britain into membership,
watched on his left by the chief negotiator,
Geoffrey Rippon, and on his right
by the foreign secretary, Douglas-Home.
He had had his way.
But it all seemed new-fangled,
just like the decimal currency
which appeared to shrink
with inflation very much faster
than the old money
whatever the genial Sir Bill Fiske (right),
in charge of the changeover, might say.

DECIMAL CURRENCY BOARD

When you go decimal shopping, remember

10/ = 50p
2/ = 10p
1/ = 5p

So sixpence equals 2½p

Everyone had trouble with the unions,
If it was not the newspaper proprietors
(left, Lords Goodman and Thomson seeking comfort at No. 10),
it was the London traffic, stopped by the TUC's marches
(below left) against the Heath government's
industrial relations bill,
which made contracts enforceable at law.
The bill took 56 days and 481 hours
of debate to pass through Parliament,
and probably worsened industrial relations
as unions fell foul of the new
National Industrial Relations Court.
The miners' national strike in January 1972,
their first since 1926, was serious.
Pickets (above right) stopped lorries moving coal
to the power stations and Fleet Street had to
put its papers to bed by lanternlight (below).
An inquiry under Lord Wilberforce
eventually gave the miners
three times the money the coal board had offered.

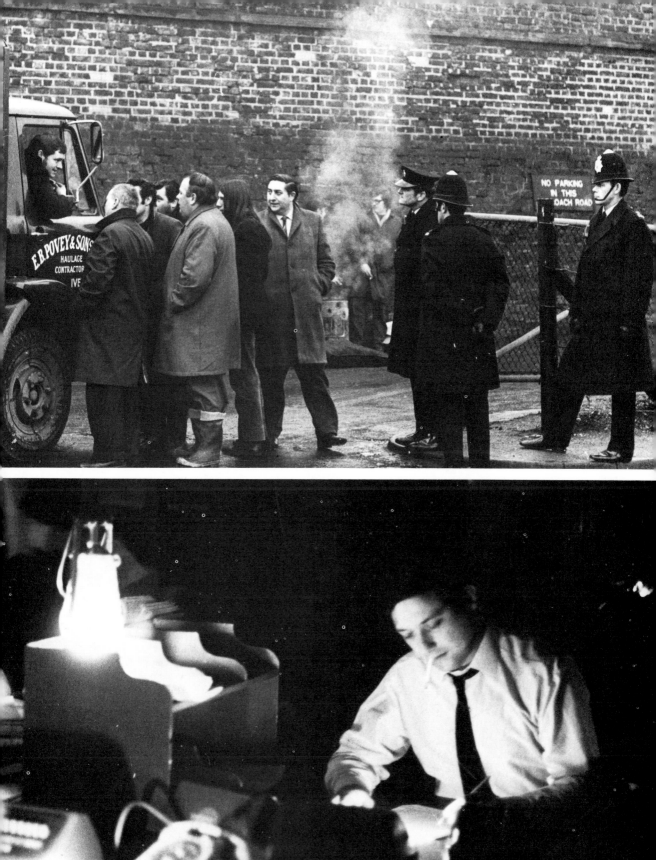

Heath was faced with rising inflation,
pushed up by rising
world commodity prices
and high wage claims.
In November 1972 he slapped on
a prices and wages freeze for 90 days.
Then, on 17 January 1973,
he announced that wages must rise
by only £1 a week
plus four per cent of present pay
at a de Gaulle-style news conference
(left) in Lancaster House.
This did not please the unions
at all
although the TUC's general secretary,
Vic Feather, and his deputy,
Len Murray (below, singing *Auld Lang Syne*
at the 1973 TUC),
were prepared to talk.
But by October,
when stage three had to be announced,

interest rates were high,
petrol prices were soaring
as a result of the Yom Kippur war,
and the unions would not do a deal.
Heath's chancellor,
after Macleod's sudden death,
was Tony Barber,
a brilliant party manager
who was not always so confident
in money matters.
It fell to him to implement
the policy of going
for rapid economic growth,
in which endemic troubles
might be eased.
The world slump of 1973–74
and the miners' second strike
ended any hope of that,
and the result of printing
more money to sustain the boom
was more inflation.

The government brought back
internment without trial
in Northern Ireland in August 1971,
allowing the round-up
of 300 suspected supporters of the IRA.
It did not go well
with the Catholic community.
Bloody Sunday in Londonderry,
when 13 Catholics were shot dead
on 30 January 1972
as paratroopers broke up
an unauthorized
civil rights demonstration,
caused even more bitterness.
Bernadette Devlin (left,
at an anti-internment meeting
in Hammersmith)
slapped the Home Secretary,
Reginald Maudling, as he sat
on the front bench in the Commons.
In the Provisional IRA's strongholds
they ran their own sort of justice
(below left) and were particularly hard
on any Catholic girl (below)
caught being friendly
with a British soldier.
For the army, with 12,000 troops
on active duty in the province,
it was a hard and unpopular job (right)
patrolling the streets.
But it had to be done.

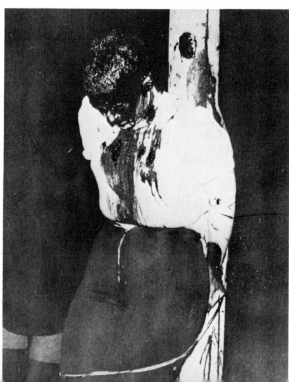

Nudity was the new name of the game,
once the Lord Chamberlain's censorship
had been abolished.
But tasteful, artistic nudity,
or nudity for nearly every taste,
was what was supplied in bulk
in *Oh! Calcutta!* (above left),
brought to London
by Kenneth Tynan (above right) in 1969.

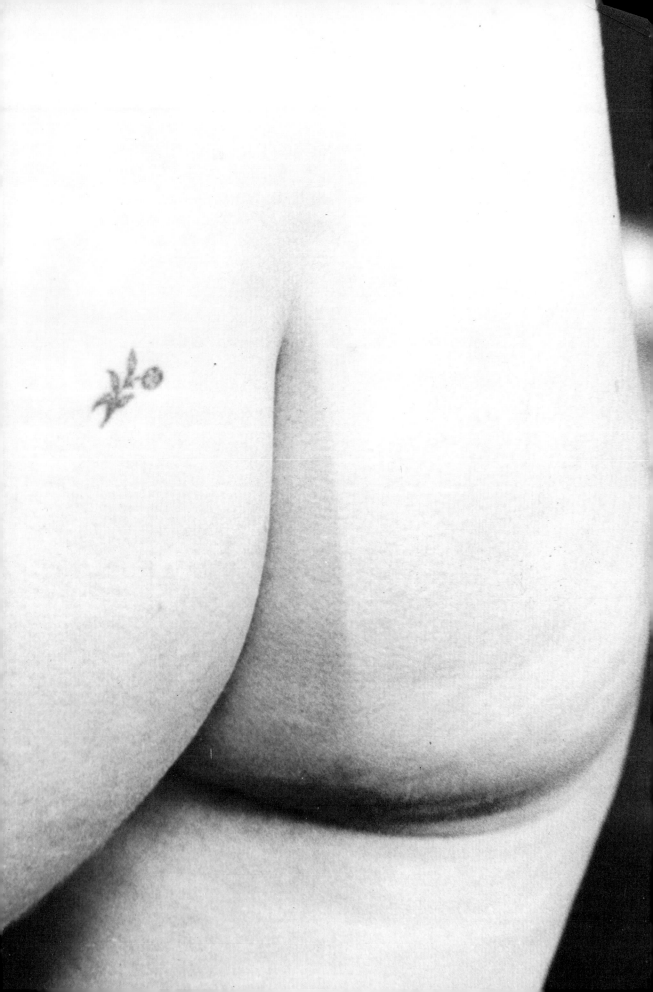

There were those, naturally,
who still wished to keep up standards.
They were led, most determinedly,
by a former art mistress, Mrs Mary Whitehouse
(above right, with guitar player Judy Mackenzie),
who developed her role from being a watchdog
of television morals into a full-scale campaigner
for the Festival of Light.
She could take no offence at the bearing
and behaviour of Captain Mainwaring
(Arthur Lowe, left), leader of the Home Guard platoon
in the gentle comedy series, *Dad's Army*, on BBC-TV.
Nor, really, at the everyday happenings
in Granada's *Coronation Street*
whose cast (above) celebrated
their tenth anniversary in January 1971.
Anathema to the right-wing brigade
were the young iconoclasts of *Oz* (right),
who won their appeal
against conviction for obscenity.
But (left to right) James Anderson, Richard Neville
and Felix Dennis had to have their hair cut
in Wormwood Scrubs.

Tony Jacklin (above, swinging) did the impossible
for a British golfer. He won
the British Open at Royal Lytham on 12 July 1969,
and the United States Open the next year.
Then he did the very possible:
never won either again.
John Conteh (left, jogging) won the world
light-heavyweight title on 1 October 1974.
Mary Peters, from Belfast (left, long-jumping),
won the gold medal in the 1972 Olympic
women's pentathlon, with a world record of 4,801 points.
Vanessa Redgrave (above) added to her reputation
in films, if not so much in very left-wing politics,
in Antonioni's critique of the 1960s, *Blow Up*.
George Best of Manchester United
and Northern Ireland, the most gifted footballer of his day,
preferred to take things too easy
too often (above right) for his later employers.
Not so easy (right): the wrestling
of Gerald and Birkin (Oliver Reed and Alan Bates)
in Ken Russell's *Women in Love*,
an adaptation of D. H. Lawrence.

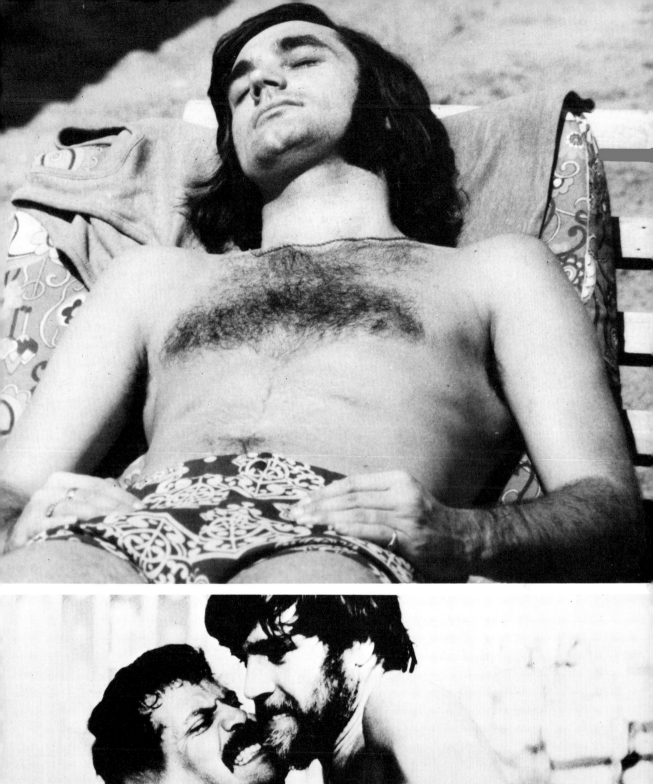

As the Conservatives grew unpopular with their voters,
the Liberals, under Jeremy Thorpe (above, with his second wife Marion,
formerly Lady Harewood), picked up a good harvest
of by-election victories at Rochdale, Sutton and Cheam,
Isle of Ely, Ripon and Berwick-on-Tweed.
The Berwick seat was lost chiefly because Lord Lambton (right)
had to resign when he was caught with a call-girl in May 1973.

He had been a junior air force minister.
He said, 'There has been no high-life vice ring,
no security leak, no blackmail, and as far as I know
no politician of any party is remotely connected with these events'.
However, the Lord Privy Seal, Lord Jellicoe,
hearing there was a stir,
confessed to an indiscretion of his own. He had to go, too.

Princess Anne, the best sportswoman the royal family has ever produced,
became an international star at three-day eventing (left),
riding for Britain at the Montreal Olympics and even in the Soviet Union.
She regularly spoke her mind to photographers who gathered to see her fall.
She married Captain Mark Phillips, another successful horseman,
at Westminster Abbey on 14 November 1973 (above).
Her brother, Prince Edward, was the page and her cousin,
Lady Sarah Armstrong-Jones, the bridesmaid.

Heath's general election, called in February 1974 to beat the miners'
second strike, ended in a stalemate;
the opinion polls had been wrong again.
Though Heath waited in No. 10, as he had every right to do, to see if he could get
enough Liberal support to carry on,
Thorpe could not get his party to agree.
So the Heath furniture (right) had to go on its travels again.
Labour was back, though hardly with the authority
to do anything except stop what Heath was doing.
Foot (above left) accepted his first ministerial job
as employment secretary. He quickly settled with the miners.
Wilson gave Castle social services and Callaghan the Foreign Office
(above right, at the one-day party conference in November).
He kept up a brisk display of activity before calling
another general election on 10 October.
This time Labour got its majority,
but only just: three over all other parties.
Wilson now had to tackle runaway inflation.
By July 1975 he had got the unions, reluctantly,

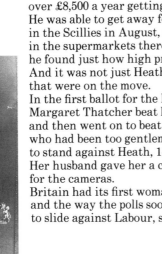

to accept a £6 limit on pay rises
(with everyone earning
over £8,500 a year getting nothing).
He was able to get away for his holidays
in the Scillies in August, although
in the supermarkets there (above)
he found just how high prices had gone.
And it was not just Heath's belongings
that were on the move.
In the first ballot for the leadership in February 1975,
Margaret Thatcher beat him, 130–119,
and then went on to beat Willie Whitelaw,
who had been too gentlemanly
to stand against Heath, 146–79.
Her husband gave her a congratulatory kiss (right)
for the cameras.
Britain had its first woman party leader,
and the way the polls soon began
to slide against Labour, she wasn't stopping at that.

Wilson had promised the country a chance
at the ballot box to see if Britain should stay in Europe.
Heath's influence with the Conservatives had slipped visibly,
but the leadership (above right) was still very much pro-market.
Whitelaw, Thatcher, Heath and Maudling could make common cause on that.
Labour, as ever, was badly split.
Wilson and Callaghan carried out a minor renegotiation of the treaty,
endorsed at Dublin (above) in March, and said they were satisfied.
Members of the cabinet were allowed to make up their own minds,
but the full strength of the government's publicity machine
seemed to have been enlisted on the Yes side.
London's votes were counted at Earl's Court (right) and the result
was a clear-cut victory for the marketeers.
Nationally, they won by 17,378,000 to 8,470,000.
Only the Shetlands and the Western Isles voted No.

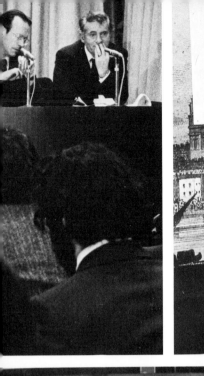

Keep Britain in Europe

st
UK North Sea oil
June 1975
others

The North Sea oil boom was on.
The energy secretary, Tony Benn, was at hand (above) when
the first 14,000 tons from the Argyll field were pumped
into BP's refinery at the Isle of Grain, in the Thames estuary.
The fabrication of oil rigs gave some needed work
to the north-east coast and to Scotland.
The £38 million platform (above right), towed out from Hartlepool

THANKS
TONY
WELL MA
IT WO

to the Thistle field in August 1976, was 606 ft high
and weighed 35,000 tons, the North Sea's biggest.
More humdrum, but just as close to Benn's heart,
were the workers' co-operatives
into which he put public money during his time
as industry secretary.
The Meriden motor-cycle factory (left) was the longest-lasting.

The summers were hot, the prisons were crowded,
and the prisoners took to breaking through to the roof
to tell everyone about their grievances.
These IRA men (above) did not like the prison-visiting rules at Wormwood Scrubs.
The Labour, and latterly English Nationalist, MP for Walsall North,
John Stonehouse (below), was sentenced to seven years for fraud at the Old Bailey.
His business affairs had got into a bad tangle
and he faked his own death when swimming at a Miami beach in 1974.
Two months later he was found in Australia and brought back in disgrace.
He served three years of his sentence.
The swing to Conservative in the ensuing by-election at Walsall North,
22.5 per cent, was the biggest of the Wilson and Callaghan governments.
Glasgow finally pulled down much of the Gorbals (above right),
replacing the old grey tenements with multi-storey flats.
Gorbals people said the planners and the builders
had taken the warmth out of the place.
Some of Glasgow's huge council estates, the biggest in Europe,
soon got a worse reputation than the Gorbals had ever had.
Glasgow's dustmen struck, saying their pay was very bad.
It was something every city now had to get used to,
as firemen, bus drivers, dustmen
and hospital porters were organized into a new militancy.

The IRA carried their bombing campaign to Britain.
They wrecked a coach carrying soldiers (left)
in February 1974, and planted other bombs
at Westminster Hall and the Tower of London,
where they blew up tourists.
Princess Anne was held up in her car
(below left) by a deranged attacker
in the Mall in March 1974.
She clung to her husband until help arrived.
Heath's new home in Belgravia
had a bomb thrown through the sitting-room window
(below) on 22 December.
He had been conducting carols at Broadstairs,
then took a cup of tea with friends
and so escaped the explosion.
Some of the neighbours complained, though.
The worst IRA bombing was in Birmingham
on the night of 22 November.

Nineteen people were killed
and 200 injured at two pubs,
the Mulberry Bush (left)
and the Tavern in the Town.
It was these deaths that hastened on
the Prevention of Terrorism Act,
giving the Home Secretary powers
that Labour's left-wingers disliked.
But the bombings soon began to die away.
There were summer droughts,
and people complained hotly.
Standpipes, always the sign of a water crisis,
began to appear in the streets
(above right, at Moortown, Leeds, in August 1976).
No one ever expected it in Britain,
but the drought actually began
to damage the foundations of some homes.
For gardeners the worst news
was that hose pipes and sprinklers were banned.
Much more welcome was the ban on washing cars.
Otherwise, everyone just lay back and enjoyed it.

Some did very well.
John Curry (below) carried off the British,
European, World and Olympic
figure skating titles in 1976.
Basil Hume, Abbot of Ampleforth school,
in Yorkshire (below right), became
Roman Catholic Archbishop of Westminster
(and, shortly after, a Cardinal)
in February 1976.
He quickly established himself
as a national figure,
active on ecumenical occasions
and was even, exaggeratedly,
suggested as a candidate for the Papacy.
For penance he said
he supported Newcastle United.
In the gossip columns' story of the year
(this time a *Daily Express* exclusive)
the authoress Lady Antonia Fraser,
wife of Sir Hugh Fraser, MP,
and daughter of the pillar
of respectability, Lord Longford,
ran off with the playwright,
Harold Pinter (above).
His wife's revenge, widely reported,
was to reveal Lady Antonia's shoe size.
The National Theatre opened
at last on 16 March 1976
in its £13 million premises
on the South Bank.
The Lyttelton, one of three theatres
(the others being the open-stage Olivier
and the small Cottesloe),
was ready first and Peter Hall,
the director, posed suitably there (right).
The Tate bought a pile of bricks (below right),
artistically arranged.
It was precisely
the sort of thing to like
if you liked that sort of thing.

The Lyttelton
Theatre

Wilson had taken
much pleasure
in being a long-lasting
prime minister,
but on 16 March 1976
he suddenly announced
he was retiring.
He said he had always meant to
when he was 60,
but there was much talk
that he saw trouble ahead.
His resignation honours list,
typed as usual by his secretary
Lady Falkender (with him, left),
contained some curious names
and brought him
immediate trouble.
Callaghan beat Foot, 176–137,
in the Labour MPs' vote
for the new leader,
and he took the call
from the Palace.
Then there was real trouble.
While Labour was at Blackpool
for its conference
in September the £1 nearly fell
off the end of the pier (right).
The chancellor, Healey,
had to turn back
from a flight to Manila
and Callaghan told the party
that it could not spend
its way out of a recession,
'The option no longer exists'.
The Queen duly
gave Wilson the Garter.

THE TIMES

Wednesday September 29 1976
No 59,821
Price twelve pence

Sterling fall halts Healey mission

Huge long-term loan preferred cure

Mr Callaghan's grim speech wins little conference applause

Violence
new car i

GUARDIAN

Wednesday September 29 1976
10p

ancels trip: urgent Bank of England talks

Britain will borrow to prop up pound

By ALEX BRUMMER, Financial Correspondent

uds warning

Rainfall chaos
in Glasgow

The Daily Telegraph

FINAL

No. 37,741. LONDON, WEDNESDAY, SEPTEMBER 29, 1976.

Printed in LONDON and MANCHESTER

8p

RISING DAMP
CAVITY WALL INSULATION

LONGINES
The World's Most Honoured Watch

Healey turns back at airport

£ FACING ROUT IN MARKETS

Statement in Lords today: import controls likely

The pound crashed again on foreign exchange markets yesterday, falling by nearly 4½ cents against the United States dollar on a day which saw Mr Healey, Chancellor of the Exchequer, turn back

STRAIGHT LEFT FOR PRENTICE

By JAMES WIGHTMAN, Political Staff

Britain sends Minister to see Smith

THE Sun

5p

Wednesday, September 29, 1976

£ CRISIS

- Disaster as the pound plunges
- Healey turns back at airport

Now the pound is worth 54p
PAGE 2

The long march has begun, says the Premier
PAGE 7

SAVE OUR STERLING!

Callaghan in a battle to stop the rot

PREMIER James Callaghan was battling last night to save the £—and the Labour Government.

By ROGER CARROLL and JAMES LEWTHWAITE

THE SUN SAYS
Jim must swing the axe!

Mr JAMES CALLAGHAN spoke yesterday — and the pound just went on plunging.

Now the Government is in a panic. Chancellor Denis Healey has scrapped his flight plans for the Far East and the Treasury is dusting off the emergency package of economic measures which it has ever handy.

Events have taken over from the politicians and they will act because they have no choice.

Jim Callaghan spoke well. But his words about Britain's disaster-bound economy were not enough.

He may have told the Labour

MINUTES

RESENTFUL

Daily Mail

WEDNESDAY, SEPTEMBER 29, 1976
7p

20-1 WINNER AND A DOUBLE FOR RICKMAN
SEE PAGE 44

Healey cancels flight at airport as crisis deepens and rumours of coalition spread

PANIC OVER THE POUND

By GORDON GREIG, Political Editor

PREMIER James Callaghan has grimly sweating out the most ferocious battering the £ has ever

The smile on the face of disaster

Daily Mirror

BRITAIN'S BIGGEST DAILY SALE

Wednesday, September 29, 1976
No 32,603

Dagenham workers go on rampage

RIOTERS

SM

UP

PLA

Fires b
—then t
turned

£ Healey in a crisis bid to save pound

THE RACE to save the crumbling pound was on last night. Chancellor Denis Healey made a dramatic turn-round at Heathrow Airport as sterling collapsed to an all-time low.

He was due to fly out for a meeting of Commonwealth finance ministers in Hong Kong.

By JOHN BUCKLAND and CHRISTOPHER BUCKLAND

RIOTING car workers went on a rampage of destruction at Ford's Dagenham works early today.

They smashed cars, attacked the security gates and started fires inside the factory.

When angry action

Conference round-up
PAGES 4 and 5
On a road to ruin
PAGE 6

DAILY EXPRESS

No. 23,720 Wednesday September 29 1976

Weather: Sunny spells, showers

Price 7p

Healey in late night search for emergency rescue package as the £ crashes again

BATTLE OF BRITAIN '76

By John Warden and Patrick Lay

A FRANTIC search for emergency policies to save the £ was going on in Whitehall last night as the Government was caught paralysed at the Labour Party conference at Blackpool.

The City was hoping that Chancellor Mr. Denis Healey—after calling off a vital trip abroad on the tarmac at Heathrow—would produce a swift plan to fight this financial Battle of Britain 1976.

Down and down despite Callaghan's warning

How Denis did his flying about-turn

Ford men in riot

Workers overturn cars

By Michael Evans

The £ and the world

Callaghan and Healey
had to ask the unions
for three things:
restraint on wages,
acceptance of public-spending cuts,
and turning a partly-blind eye
to the rapid rise in unemployment.
Healey's budget
in April 1976
actually offered tax cuts
if the unions
would keep wages down.
The left did not like
any of this (left),
but a special TUC congress
voted in June to keep
the average wage rise to 4.5
per cent. It was a useful start.
The miners' president,
Joe Gormley (left),
kept his militants
and communists under control.
So did the transport workers'
Jack Jones (below left)
even when attacked
for giving in
to the government too easily.
But Jones was reaching retirement
and his successor, Moss Evans,
was less able, or willing,
to restrain the left
just to keep Labour in office.
The face of the TUC's general secretary,
Len Murray (below),
grew longer and more drawn.
British soccer fans
became notorious in Europe
for exporting their familiar hooliganism
although, as Manchester United
found at St Etienne
in September 1977 (top right),
the police were not
as friendly as at home.
Scotland went off
to the World Cup in Argentina
in 1978 the only British team
and high in hopes.
'We're on the march
with Ally's army,'
the fans sang.
But it turned out that Scotland
and their manager,
Ally Macleod, could not
even beat lowly Iran (right).
One Scottish player
was found taking drugs,
and the team returned chastened—
until the next time.

Jeremy Thorpe was in the toils.
Rumour and suspicion grew around him while he worked
in his office as Liberal leader (opposite).
He had been accused by Norman Scott,
a male model (left), of having a homosexual relationship
and of having one of Scott's dogs, Rinka, shot as a warning;
there was the suggestion that Scott's own life was threatened.
All this Thorpe steadily denied:
to his friends, to Liberal MPs and to the public.
But there were details that were hard to explain away,
especially an affectionate note from Thorpe to Scott
saying, 'Bunnies can (and will) go to France .. I miss you'.
In May 1976 Thorpe resigned the leadership,
complaining of a 'campaign of denigration'.
In August 1978 Thorpe and three other men
were charged with conspiracy to murder;
Thorpe himself was also charged
with incitement to murder.
The 1979 general election arrived
before the case could be heard.
Thorpe, almost waxen-faced in the television camera's eye,
heard he had been beaten in North Devon by 8,473,
after being its MP for 20 years.
Five days later he stood in the dock at the Old Bailey.
It was not until 22 June
that he heard the foreman of the jury,
who had been out for nearly 52 hours,
say, 'Not guilty'.
He appeared on the balcony of his home (below)
with his mother and his wife, an innocent man.

The Queen and her people
celebrated her silver jubilee
on 7 June 1977.
She and the Duke set off in the coach
in which she had ridden to her coronation (far left)
for the thanksgiving service
at St Paul's,
watched by millions around the world
on BBC television.
ITV was on strike.
The crowds were with her all the way
and they stayed outside the Palace (left)
until well into the night.
It was a time for loyal street parties
all over the country (below left,
near the Elephant and Castle,
in south-east London).
The most loyal streets
were working-class ones.
The Queen reviewed her fleet,
including its last two aircraft carriers,
Ark Royal (below foreground) and *Hermes*,
and the ships of the Nato navies,
off Portsmouth.
She went, too, to Glasgow,
Cardiff and Northern Ireland, despite the IRA,
to share in their celebrations.

British sportspeople began to do better.
Geoffrey Boycott agreed to forgive Test cricket and return
to England's side in 1977, immediately scoring a century (above left)
against the Australians at Trent Bridge.
He scored another against them, his 100th century,
in the next match at his home ground, Headingley.
Virginia Wade won Wimbledon in 1977 (above), after what seemed a lifetime's trying.
Her fans willed her to beat Betty Stove 4–6, 6–3, 6–1.
Partly because the Americans weren't there,
Britain won more gold medals than expected at the Moscow Olympics in 1980.
Duncan Goodhew (right) won the 100 metres breaststroke.
On the track Steve Ovett won the 800 metres (above right),
with Sebastian Coe second. Coe then went on to win the 1500 metres.

Signs of the 'seventies. Lord Rosebery put up
Mentmore's treasures for auction in May 1977,
to help him pay £3 million in taxes (above).
He did so well, and so did the auctioneers, Christie's,
that other financially-embarrassed aristocrats followed suit.
Princess Margaret was increasingly seen around town
not only with her daughter but, usually at a discreet distance (below),
with her friend Roddy Llewellyn.
The gossip columns thrived on it, but it was not viewed
with complete approval elsewhere in the family.
The first baby fertilized in a test tube, Louise Joy Brown,

FISH & CHIPS
SOLD
HERE

يوجد
عندنا لحم حلال
مذبوح على الشريعه
الإسلاميه

was born on 25 July 1978 at Oldham general hospital.
Louise weighed 5 lb 12 oz and appeared (below right)
with her physiologist and gynaecologist friends.
Fast food arrived from America with the McDonald's hamburger counters,
Colonel Sanders Kentucky-fried chicken and their imitators.
And, with the influx of Arabs and Iranians into London,
even the oldest of fast-food signs had to be translated (above).
The kebabs were coming.
In nationalist Scotland, personified by Margo MacDonald (below),
and Wales they thought home rule was coming in 1979.
It wasn't.

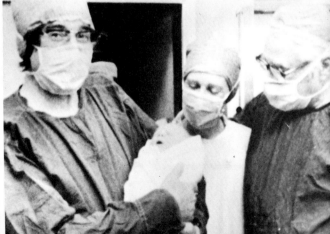

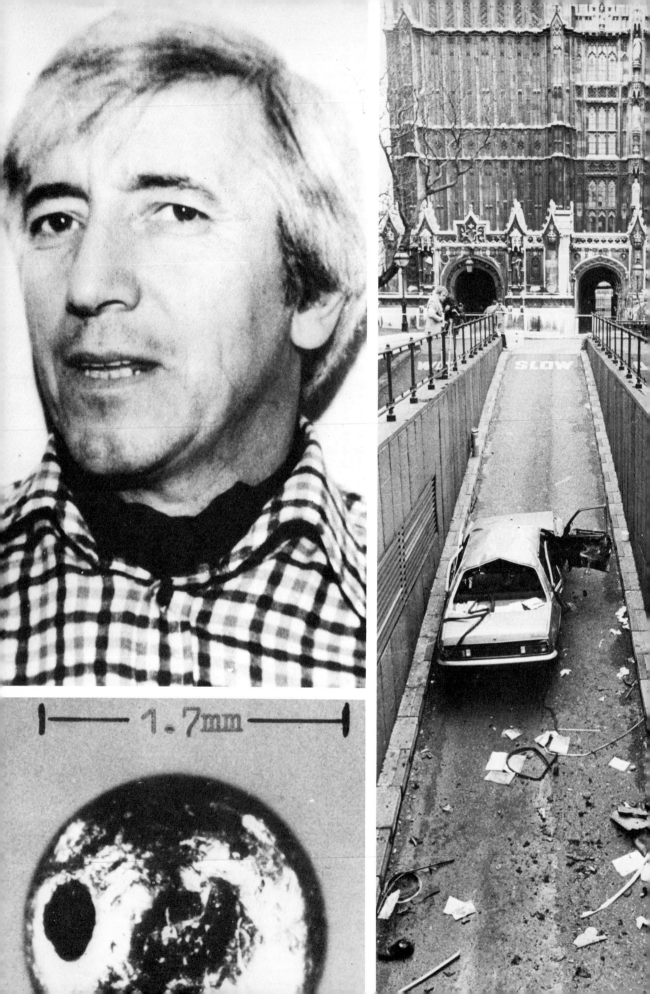

An exile from communist Bulgaria,
Georgi Markov (far left), was murdered
in London in September 1978
when, it appeared, he was stabbed
in the thigh by the point
of an umbrella
while standing at a bus stop.
A poisoned pellet, slightly smaller
than a pinhead, was found (below, far left)
in Markov's thigh.
It had two holes, drilled at right angles.
Scotland Yard said that a similar pellet
had been found in the back
of another Bulgarian defector
who was attacked in Paris.
The Conservative spokesman
on Northern Ireland, Airey Neave,
was killed on 30 March 1979
when a bomb attached to his car
exploded as he drove out
of the House of Commons
underground car park (left).
It was a bad blow to Mrs Thatcher,
whose staunch adviser and ally he had been.
The IRA blew up the boat
in which Lord Mountbatten and his family
were fishing in Donegal Bay on 27 August.
His grandsons (right), Philip,
Norton and Michael Knatchbull
and Ashley Hicks,
marched in the funeral procession
to Westminster Abbey.
His charger, Dolly (below right),
which he had last ridden
at the Trooping the Colour,
was led in the procession
with his boots reversed in the stirrups.

The pinstripe was back in fashion—for some.
Michael Edwardes, the determined new chairman of British Leyland (below left),
set out to get government financial backing, discipline the workforce, and launch
what he hoped would be his worldbeater, the Mini-Metro.
The television comedy hit, *Are You Being Served?*,
was set in a big department store, one of the disappearing dinosaurs of the high street.
The series starred (below) Frank Thornton as Captain Peacock
and John Inman as the camp Mr Humphries.

Peter Sellers's Inspector Clouseau series filled the cinemas, giving Sellers
the opportunity to try out every comic disguise he could imagine,
including (below) a Mafia outfit in *Revenge of the Pink Panther*.
His death in 1980 was a great loss.
James Callaghan favoured the style for his annual appearance,
with Margaret Thatcher (below), in the House of Lords for the Queen's Speech.
Few Queen's Speeches, whichever prime minister wrote them,
could offer anything much except higher taxes.

Another mole, friend of Burgess,
Maclean and Philby, was unearthed many years after
the authorities had first discovered his burrowing,
in the person of Sir Anthony Blunt (above, at Hampton Court).
He had been looking after the Queen's pictures
since confessing.
There was, of course,
a great to-do about the establishment
looking after its own.

The newly-appointed Archbishop of Canterbury,
the Right Reverend Robert Runcie,
a former tank officer,
was shown a gargoyle of himself
at St Albans cathedral,
his old diocese.

ve you ever wished you were better informed?
THE TIMES

Activity Books

Paperback £1 each

The management of *The Times* and the *Sunday Times* went into battle
with the printing unions over bringing in what was called 'new technology';
that was, replacing the Victorian-style technology
by which Fleet Street was still creakingly produced.
It was hoped this would stop the losses that were draining
any interest the young Lord Thomson, in Toronto, had in the papers.
After a year's shutdown the Thomson management gave in.
Lord Thomson sold to the Australian,
Rupert Murdoch, for £12 million on 12 February 1981.

Nureyev finally got to dance
with Miss Piggy, heroine of *The Muppet Show*,
in the ATV studios at Boreham Wood.
Jim Henson's puppets
were in production in October 1977
with sales all round the world.

Up and up went Margaret Thatcher.
The Callaghan government faced a vote of no-confidence
on 28 March 1979.
The Conservatives were joined by 32 MPs
from the minor parties,
all with grievances,
and the government was beaten, 311–310.
It was the first time a government had fallen
in a Commons vote since Ramsay MacDonald's
minority Labour government 55 years before.
Thatcher was a tireless campaigner.
She went shopping to show (far left) what Tory pounds
had bought and how little Labour ones did.
She had herself hauled aloft by the marines (left).
And on the night of 3 May,
at Tory party headquarters
(above, with her husband behind her and her son on her left),
she heard she had won with a swing of 5.1 per cent.
She had appealed to the Britain
'which may not make the daily news
but which each one of us knows'.
That Britain had its first woman prime minister.

Thatcher had seemed, at times,
to sympathize with Ian Smith's
new solution for Zimbabwe-Rhodesia:
government by the moderate Bishop Abel Muzorewa.
But she agreed at the Commonwealth conference
at Lusaka (left, with the Queen)
in August 1979
that efforts should be made
to bring in the black guerrillas,
the boys in the bush.
Their leaders, Robert Mugabe
and Joshua Nkomo (below),
sat together as the Patriotic Front
at the Lancaster House conference
that began in September.
They were uneasy allies,
but got enough of their way
to agree to elections.
When the result was known on 4 March 1980,
Mugabe had won a resounding victory.
The Prince of Wales flew
to the independence celebrations
and received (right,
with the governor, Lord Soames)
the Union Jack that had flown
for the last time at Government House, Salisbury.

The Iranian embassy in London was seized
by dissident Iranian gunmen in May 1980.
They held hostage 19 of the staff,
a British policeman,
Trevor Lock, and two BBC men for six days.
Iranian students,
loyal to the Ayatollah Khomeini in Teheran,
prayed in Kensington road,
at a safe distance (above);
but it was the Special Air Service
that settled things, going in with automatics
and stun grenades (left).
The hostages were freed;
all but one of the gunmen were shot.

The National Front caused the police much trouble
(with much overtime pay, too)
by its marches (above) through preponderantly black districts.
After fighting at Lewisham and in Birmingham,
chief constables became more inclined
to apply to have provocative marches banned.
The Front fought 303 seats in the 1979 election,
securing all of 191,700 votes
and losing all 303 deposits.
John Lennon, of the Beatles (left), was shot dead
outside his home in New York by a gunman
who had apparently stalked him for days.
His admirers mourned him
as the voice of their generation.

Callaghan, tired of Labour's wranglings
(right, at the Blackpool conference),
stepped down from the leadership
on 15 October 1980.
He was 68 and, unique in the century,
had held all four
of the highest posts in government.
The Labour conference had voted
to add trade union and constituency party votes
to the MPs' when it came
to choosing a new leader.
But when the MPs voted for Michael Foot
(right, with suitably injured right foot),
beating Healey 139–129,

the left wing were happy anyway.
The unhappy ones formed what was called
the gang of three who then,
with Roy Jenkins on 25 January 1981
(left to right: William Rodgers,
Shirley Williams, Jenkins, David Owen),
set up the Council for Social Democracy
and a new party on 26 March.
Other MPs joined them.
The Liberal leader, Steel (right),
hoped they would join him,
at least in an electoral pact but talks,
though friendly,
were slow to get far.

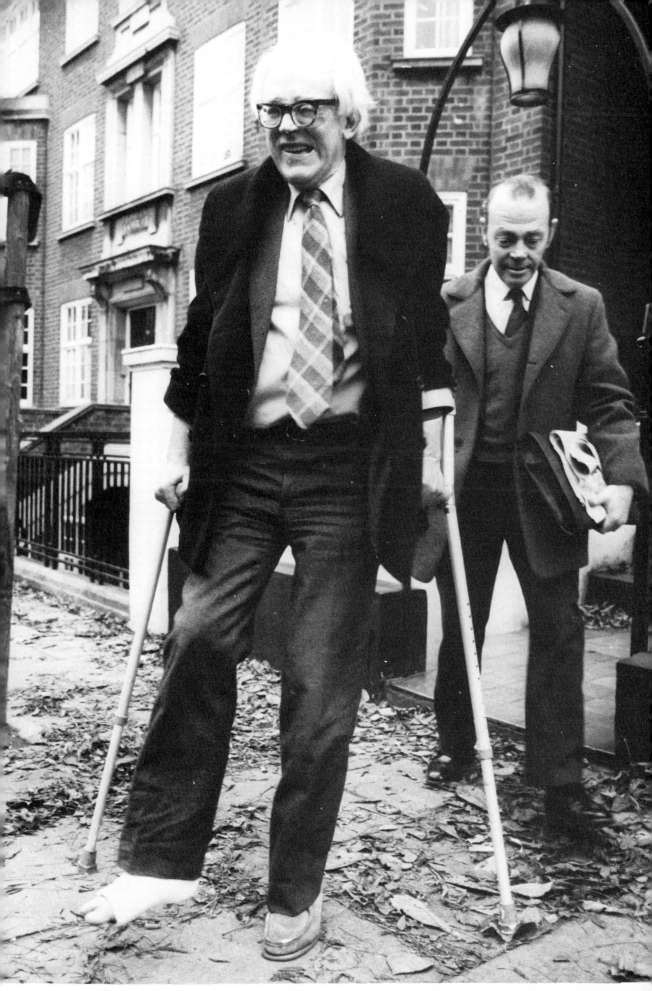

Margaret Thatcher was very much
the boss in her cabinet.
She removed the dandruff
from the shoulder
of the Leader of the House,
Norman St John-Stevas (left);
and removed him from office entirely
in her first reshuffle in January 1981.
She had to try to keep in step
two very different groups of ministers.
There were those,
chiefly dealing with economic affairs,
who admired the rigorous views
of the industry secretary,
Sir Keith Joseph (above left).
Unhappily for Sir Keith he had to confess
the government's failure
to control public spending
in its first 18 months
and regularly announce public subsidies
to beleaguered state industries,
such as BL, BR and BSC.
Other ministers, who had been close to Heath,
were less ideological,
more pragmatic,
when it came to difficult decisions.
The prime minister called them 'wets',
especially the employment secretary,
Jim Prior (above right),
but he went on with his views undented.
She would not admit to U-turns in policy.
'The lady's not for turning',
she told the 1980 Conservative conference.
But she had troubles.
The money supply was harder to manage
than she had thought,
the unions were restive about cuts,
and unemployment
moved up toward 3 million.

Index
of people